IT'S A shareable LIFE·

A PRACTICAL GUIDE ON SHARING

by Chelsea Rustrum, Gabriel Stempinski, Alexandra Liss

First published 2014
It's a Sharable Life
by Chelsea Rustrum, Gabriel Stempinski, Alexandra Liss
©2014 Chelsea Rustrum, Gabriel Stempinski, Alexandra Liss

Book Cover Design: Audrey Jardin
Book Layout Designer: Ramesh Kumar Pitchai

ISBN 978-0-9904891-7-7 (Paperback)
ISBN 978-0-9904891-6-0 (Digital)
(United States of America)

TABLE OF CONTENTS

Part One: Why Share?...11
    Why Share?...13
    Sharing is Not So New...14
    Stranger Danger...17
    Access Changes Everything...19
    The Digital Rebirth of Sharing.......................................22
    Why Should You Share?...26

Part Two: Learn How to Share..29
    A Definition for the Sharing Economy............................30
    How to Read this Book...32

Part Three: Shareable Guides...33

Shareable Stuff..35
    A Case for Being Neighborly..41
    "Been sleeping on the floor for a year" A Craiglist Story......44
    How to Get a Free Couch (or Anything Else) on Craigslist......45
    How to Score Free Stuff on Freecycle..............................49
    How to Get a Shareable Prom Dress................................60
    How to Swap Your Clothes and Always Have a New Outfit......63
    How to "Pay it Forward" Using Facebook.......................68
    Other Ways to Share Stuff...71

Shareable Food..75
    How to Share a Meal in Your Home.................................78
    How to Create a Free Farm Stand in Your Community......81
    How to Set Up an Urban Farm for Sharing Food.............87
    Other Shareable Food Services..94

Shareable Travel...99
    How to Travel in Style Using Airbnb...............................103
    "Airbnb helped us create our business".........................112
    How to Tour with the Locals...114
    How to Travel the World on a Backpacker Budget...........119
    How to Travel for Free and Learn How to Farm Organically......131
    How to Swap Your Home for the Holiday of a Lifetime......136
    Other Fun Ways to Share Travel.....................................142

Shareable Education...145
    How to Take Free Ivy League Courses Online.................150
    How to Take a Course on Any Subject............................155
    How to Create a Course on Any Subject and Get Paid with Udemy.com......158
    "I made $200-400 an hour for sharing my knowledge".....162
    How to Share Your Skills Online and Get Paid................164
    How to Share Time and Skills With Your Neighbors........170
    How to Participate in a Local Time Bank........................173
    What's Next in Shareable Education?..............................176

Shareable Creativity 179
How to Crowdfund Your Dreams 183
How to Use and Share Digital Media 195
How to Turn an Idea into an Invention 206
"It's a Shareable Life" Book Cover 212
How to Crowdsource Graphic Design 214
How to Share Your Handmade Goods and Crafts and Get Paid 218
The Future of Shareable Creativity 225

Shareable Transportation 229
Shareable Cars 232
How to Make $300 a Month by Renting Out Your Car 234
"I earn cash for grad school by renting out my car" 241
How to Take a Free Road Trip 242
How to "Hitchhike" Safely 248
How to Ditch Your Car Using the Sharing Economy 252
The Future of Shareable Transportation 255

Shareable Work 259
How to Work From Anywhere 261
How Andrew Took His Business to the Next Level by Trading Spaces 265
How to Share Office Space by Coworking 267
The Power of Coworking 274
The TaskRabbit Story 276
How to Make Extra Money When You're Underemployed 278
"The right work at the right time" 285
Other Options for Shareable Work 287

Shareable Home 291
How to Live Rent-Free by Hosting Guests 293
"How I lived rent free using Airbnb" 304
How to Setup a Coliving House 307
How to Share Your Parking Spot 319
Other Ways to Share Your Home 324

Living a Shareable Life 327
Sharing for a Flexible Lifestyle 328
A Shareable Household 332
Sharing to Create Luck 336
Using the Sharing Economy to Get Out of Debt 338
Sharing to Travel More 340
"Nick Just Wants to Help" 342

Final Thoughts 347
Dedication 350
About the Authors 353

Foreword

By Neal Gorenflo

Warning. This book will change your life.

I knocked nervously on the door. I didn't know what was on the other side of it except what I had learned from the online profile of my Airbnb host, Terry.

I heard a few locks click on this Brooklyn loft. Terry opened the door. We greeted each other awkwardly. She too only knew me from my online profile and a few e-mails we had exchanged. Otherwise, we were total strangers. And I would be living with her for five days.

My nervousness vanished when shortly thereafter she gestured to her fridge and said, "Would you like a beer?" That sounded pretty good after a day of security checks, bad food, and cramped seating on my flight from San Francisco to New York. She was speaking my language.

I set my luggage aside, and we sat down to chat over beers on the picnic table in her kitchen just steps from the front door. She asked about my trip. I told her that I was traveling to attend a conference about the sharing economy, and that I had co-founded a nonprofit in 2009, Shareable, with the mission to empower everyone to share. I explained that the experience we were having was part of a much broader phenomenon, and that we focused on getting more people started in this way of life.

Halfway through our beer, she asked if I was hungry. She had just made a fresh batch of organic vegetarian chili. I said yes, I was starved. Plus, I didn't feel like going out after a long day of travel. She heated up the chili. It was delicious.

Over chili, I asked about her place. She explained that she's an architect, and that she designed the interior herself. The inspiration to build a cabin inside of her loft came from a desire to create a separate, private space in an otherwise wall-less loft. Her friends rallied to build out the interior of the space, including another bedroom, using two by fours and plywood. It was attractive, yet unpolished. It reminded me of my uncle Donald's hand-built cabin in Winchendon, Massachusetts where I spent many a summer. Like my uncle's cabin, the personality of the resident was expressed in every beam and joist. I felt at home in the quirky imperfection.

The cabin in the loft also played a role in her career. Her employer had recently reduced her hours, she was doing more freelance work, and her income was less steady. Renting the cabin on Airbnb added to her financial security, and at the same time it gave her some freedom to pursue projects that were more aligned with her interests.

After Terry bussed our chili bowls, she asked if I'd like a brownie. I already had a cold craft beer, delicious chili, and now she was offering me homemade chocolate brownies? I couldn't believe my good luck. I was bowled over by Terry's hospitality, and naturally said yes.

Over brownies, I asked about her neighborhood. She recommended Roberta's, locally famous for their brick oven pizza. And she gave me another half-dozen suggestions for places to check out. I made the rounds, and spurred on by my connection with Terry, made a point of connecting with other locals. The following night, I struck up a conversation with a bartender at Fatty 'Cue, and he introduced me – gratis – to a locally famous concoction, the Pickleback, which is a shot of whiskey chased by a shot of pickle brine. Whoa, let me tell you, that will wake you up. Not exactly my thing, but it was a welcome initiation – "you're in my 'hood, and this is what we drink, here you go…"

It was on this footing that I began a five day stay in New York City. It was hands down the best reception I've gotten anywhere, anytime. No hotel has ever come close. And it made all the difference. It framed my whole visit in an incredibly positive way, and this goodness spilled over into other experiences in New York that were not connected, except by me.

What's even more remarkable is that this kind of experience is common in the shareable life. My use of Airbnb on this trip was part of a year-long life experiment that I blogged in 2011 called, The Year of Living Shareably. I had similarly empowering social encounters sharing cars, childcare, and more during some 30 sharing experiments I tried that year. And while I didn't do this life experiment to save money, I ended up saving my family approximately $17,000 that year. This is the opportunity that's before us today, to create incredible life experiences for each other, make better use of our resources, and save a ton of cash.

Inexperienced, and without a guide, I stumbled through that year of exploring the sharing economy. Now you have a guide!

It's a Shareable Life will expertly guide you through your adventure with a lot less confusion. Because of the positive experiences and practical benefits I got from going fully shareable, I can't recommend this lifestyle and book highly enough. The authors, who I all know, are hardcore sharers themselves. They painstakingly created this guide with the goal of forever changing your life for the better. They want to help you create the same magic in your life that they've created in theirs. If you're not ready for a better life, then put this book down immediately. If you are, then you only need to turn the page.

Neal Gorenflo
Founder of Shareable

Part One:
Why Share?

WHY SHARE?

Good question. Perhaps we've forgotten who we are, where we came from, or even how to relate with one another?

Here are a few thoughts to ponder:

- ▶ Sharing is primal - our survival has always depended on our ability to collect resources and distribute them. Ecosystems, in fact, thrive on interdependence.

- ▶ Just because we can live in oversized houses in gated communities, with food delivered on-demand doesn't make us immune to needing one another.

- ▶ Consumerism encourages us to hoard, cram storage units full of possessions, and otherwise indebt our future with the empty promise of a better life.

- ▶ The newfound wealth of the post-Industrial Revolution doesn't seem to be making us happy. With over 25% of the U.S. population over 18 suffering from a diagnosable mental illness in a given year, our culture is clearly an overly anxious, depressed bunch. Why is that so?

The sharing economy represents a fundamental shift in the way that people interact and transact. Enabled by technology, people are now able to help one another get their needs met in a modern way.

In this book, we will take you on a journey through the recent history of sharing, perceived stranger danger, how access changes everything, and what we see as the digital rebirth of sharing. Then we will show you how to lead a Shareable Life where you'll have richer experiences, more money, and a renewed faith in humanity.

SHARING IS NOT SO NEW

We've lived in culture of sharing in all of recorded history, and even if we go back a century we were sharing. The last 100 years are the exception rather than the rule - consumerism is what's new to modern life.

Let's take a little trip down memory lane.

In Middle America during World War II, the American government imposed rationing in order to supply sufficient bullets, beans, and bandages to our soldiers overseas. This rationing resulted in families having to share commodities and create cottage industries in order to supplement income and provide for themselves and their communities. The government also used propaganda campaigns to put pressure on families to engage in car sharing, rationing, victory gardens, resource sharing, and home industry. It was the patriotic thing to do

and, under those dire circumstances, the right thing to do.

These campaigns were very successful and certainly contributed to our eventual victory. But they also helped create a mindset for novel forms of production, resource sharing, community activism, and conservation.

As America returned to post-war normalcy, the spirit of cooperation and sharing continued. The sense of community and trust amongst people was at an all-time high. It was the age of neighborhood barbecues, gardening clubs, community charities, bake sales, and general good will. Across the back fence neighbors borrowed pruning shears, cups of sugar, and socket wrenches. In many communities people didn't even bother locking their doors at night.

Then vs. Now

In 1955 the median household income in the U.S. was around $5,000 per year which, adjusted for inflation, is about $43,000 in 2013 dollars. Today's median income is just over $51,000 in the U.S. Looking at those two numbers, it would seem that the 1950s should have been a decade of poverty and struggle instead of being what is widely considered to be America's Golden Age.

Here's an interesting example. According to U.S. Census data taken in 2012 vs. the 1950s houses seem to keep growing in size.

In the 1950s	Now
1000 square foot house	2,306 square foot house
3.5 people per house hold	2.6 people per household

So we're essentially buying more than double the amount of housing for 30% fewer people.

Are we spending more money on stuff to put into our bigger, emptier houses, all of which spreads our dollars thinner and thinner? This appears counterintuitive, especially when we consider all the incredible advances that have been made since our grandparents' time.

Shouldn't we be richer as we become more advanced? Shouldn't we have figured out how to use this technology to make our lives easier, more efficient, and more fulfilling? Could it be in part because we've gone from a shared economy to an individuated economy?

We've shifted away from an economic model that included community sharing, home industry, efficiency, conservation, capital (stuff you own that helps you make money), and currency (money) to a nearly exclusive capital and currency based economy.

You don't need to watch the evening news to know that there is a deep dissatisfaction running rampant through our society, despite our relative wealth and high standard of living compared with much of the world (remember the staggering stat on mental illness in the U.S. at the beginning of the book?)

So, what's today's citizen to do? Can we use some of the real world practices from our grandparents' day to help bring about more prosperity?

We think so - keep reading!

Stranger Danger

One of the reasons that people often scoff at the idea of sharing their apartment or their car is the threat of the unknown - the threat of the stranger. What might they steal or break? Will they take advantage of the situation? How might they put us in danger?

We live in a society that is riddled with messages of fear. We're afraid of sharks, spiders, and snakes - just to name a few.

Let's look at this. In the year 2000 there were 79 reported shark attacks worldwide. Of those 79 attacks, there were 11 fatalities. With millions of beach goers entering the oceans every year, the number of shark attacks is obviously minuscule - yet, how many of us are deathly afraid of sharks?

Now, let's look at man's best friend. In 2010 the average number of people treated for dog attacks in the U.S. was 1,000 per day. So why don't we run screaming anytime a dog is spotted roaming free in a park like we would if someone at the beach saw a shark fin in the water? The answer is simple. We fear the unknown and we react to it with emotion instead of logic.

Somehow, society's fear of strangers has suffered the same fate as sharks.

And the Stranger Danger campaigns of the '70s and '80s didn't help either. Surely it's good to teach your five-year-old some common sense, but we've taken it to such an extreme level that it's becoming more difficult to even say hello to a stranger without them thinking that you have some ulterior motive. Our sense of community has slowly dissolved into a culture of us vs. them.

Fact check: According to the October 2002 study on abducted children by the Department of Justice's Office of Juvenile Justice and Delinquency Prevention, on average about 69,000 children are abducted every year in the U.S., and about 94% or 64,860 of these abductions are by family members or acquaintances. Stranger danger indeed.

How about a sharing economy example?

What do you think would happen if you let a hundred total strangers who you met on the internet stay in your house with you for the night? Not all at once, of course. Say, two people per week for a year, minus your two-week vacation. How many times do you think you would get robbed, assaulted, or otherwise harmed? If you're like the average American you're probably envisioning some pretty dismal numbers. However, members of Couchsurfing.org (all 9 million of them) do this very thing on a very regular basis and, according to their statistics of reported "Negative Experiences," you wouldn't have a single bad thing happen to you. In fact they say only a tiny fraction of one percent of their experiences turn out negative, and most of those are for relatively minor reasons.

As of 2014, the authors of this book have personally hosted over 600 complete strangers from all over the world, all without incident or issue.

Through our experiences, and those of others, the authors of this book hope to set you at ease about using the sharing economy, given it's internal safeguards and community-based review systems.

ACCESS CHANGES EVERYTHING

If you are about 30, you remember a time before the internet and cell phones. Your parents would remember a time before microwave ovens, computers and color TV. Your grandparents would recall a time before TV, and your great-grandparents would remember a time before air travel, freeways, nuclear weapons, and radio. That's just 100 years' worth of progress.

What made this particular century so different? In a word, *access*. Access to knowledge, resources, tools, and services is the foundation of this extraordinary progress. Inventors during this time were able to stand on the shoulders of earlier works to improve, expand, and repurpose them to create unprecedented technological advances.

Ownership and Access Models

Even though access is what has motivated much technological progress, society currently operates under what could be called "the ownership model." This is where a single entity owns specific knowledge, resources, tools, and/or services. Generally, only the owner reaps the benefits.

In contrast, "the access model" provides instead for knowledge, resources, tools, and services to be made freely available so that other people and groups can partake in, and contribute to the betterment of the product, industry, or community.

Some examples of ownership costs vs. the access desired:

Owning a car costs approximately $9,150 per year on average or $763 per month.

▶ Access desired: flexible transportation.

Buying a drill costs $50 and gets used 6-20 minutes in its life.

▶ Access desired: the hole in the wall to hang a picture.

Purchasing designer cocktail dress often costs upwards of $400 and is typically worn only once.

▶ Access desired: looking stylish on a night out.

Keeping your own lawnmower costs an average of $300 and is used twice a month.

▶ Access desired: a manicured lawn.

With the access model, the focus is more on what you want to accomplish and less on possessing the object of desire. If you can get what you want without owning the car, drill, dress or lawnmower, you'll have less stuff to worry about and more money in your pocket. The sharing economy is built on the access model.

Access and the internet

How about an example of access we can all relate to?

In the late '60s the Department of Defense funded a computer network called ARPANET that initially connected institutions such as UCLA, U.C. Santa Barbara and Stanford. In the beginning, the internet was mostly used by engineers, librarians, military personnel, and universities. Home offices did not exist and there was no such thing as the personal computer. The general public didn't get access to what would later be called the World Wide Web until 1995.

Today, no one owns the biggest economy in the world (the internet), but everyone has access to it.

Imagine if the Department of Defense had kept ownership over the ARPANET instead of allowing access to universities and then to the rest of the world?

As it turns out, the internet is the greatest sharing platform of all - and in fact, is a big part of what enables us to more efficiently lead shareable lives.

THE DIGITAL REBIRTH OF SHARING

While war and hardship might have inspired sharing in times past, the paradigm is shifting again - only this time we have a powerful new tool, the internet.

The World Wide Web provided a simple communications system with email, bulletin boards (much like today's forums) and chat. Integrated payment systems tipped the scales and made e-commerce such as Ebay and Amazon possible. Next, file sharing made sharing digital assets quick and easy - music, movies, books and software were among the first things to be shared online.

Once e-commerce and file sharing were going strong, we turned everyone in the world into a media outlet, a reporter and a brand. People began to blog, share socially, collaborate and have open, public conversations and personal profiles. Social media was born.

Today, we can put our trust in people that we have never met. This helps us feel more comfortable meeting and sharing stuff with strangers. Now, we build trust and reputations through the social status we create through networks, connections, reviews, and our respective "Googability."

With the amount of public exposure the internet provides, social media has created a circle of trust. Who wants a bad review or a negative blog post to tarnish their reputation forevermore? This might ruin their chances of getting a date, a job or even a loan in the future.

The drivers of the sharing economy

Why now?

While sharing isn't so new, the way we're sharing today is. Technology, money, a down economy, the millenials, urbanization, and our very biology have come to an intersection where sharing is the best option: a way to create more value, produce less debt, save the mortgage, remain employed, have flexibility, be more efficient with stuff, and connect more deeply to others.

Let's look at little closer at the drivers of the sharing economy:

Technology

Efficient sharing exists because technology has connected all of us. Our devices, networks, and marketplaces have reached a point where they are ubiquitous. Accessibility helps us make matches between needs and wants in real time. Now instead of trading a chicken for rice with the family down the road, we can trade with anyone, any time, and for any reason, using technology as the connecting point.

Money (micro-entrepreneurship)

People are motivated to share their idle assets and resources in exchange for cash or the promise of saving money. The sharing economy essentially creates micro-entrepreneurs. Now everyday people can become hoteliers, cab drivers, car rental agencies, professors and personal assistants and all without the huge investment of time, training, certification or education typically required to get started.

A down economy

Before the Great Recession, millennials were promised home ownership and economic independence if they earned college degrees and got good jobs. These turned out to be half-truths. Education is costly, entry-level jobs are hard to come by, and the promise of owning a home is moving farther and farther from reach.

Millennials

Being flashy and materialistic has increasingly lost it's luster - especially with young people. Millennials are more likely to rent instead of purchasing homes, use public transportation, and access television, clothing, and music via technology. This generation is going carless, sharing their apartments with weary travelers, crowdfunding their dreams, and helping their neighbors. They are finding solace in the network - identity in their connectedness.

Urbanization

People are gravitating to metropolitan areas. According to the U.S. Census Bureau, 81% of American citizens already reside in urban areas. With population density increasing, there will be less and less space for possessions and vehicles. Cities are the perfect platforms for sharing. From libraries to public transportation, civic services are more efficient in cities.

Our biology

And what inspires the movement toward sharing on an even deeper level? Our biology, of course! There are countless scientific studies that show that we get a kick of oxytocin (the cuddle hormone) every time we share something that someone likes on Facebook. Just as sharing information online feels good, the same is true when we share our stuff or our time with another - only our biological response is even stronger.

WHY SHOULD YOU SHARE?

We're convinced that sharing will make you happier, keep more money in your pocket, enable a flexible lifestyle, reduce your debt, and restore your faith in humanity.

The benefits of leading a Shareable Life:

You will be happier

The authors of this book have discovered firsthand how experimenting with the sharing economy gives them the high of human connection. Unlike digital forms of sharing such as poking, liking, and tweeting, the sharing economy gives people the ability to help one another get their needs met offline, oftentimes through face-to-face interactions, which many studies show, people are starved for.

You will have more money

Since much of the sharing economy cuts out the middleman by helping individuals exchange value with one another, there is more money to go around. Plus, there are many networks and marketplaces within the sharing economy where the systems rely on the currency of the gift or the pay-it-forward mentality.

You will have a more flexible lifestyle

Leaving for a trip? Great! Rent your place to someone who needs accommodation. Is your car parked on the street during the day? Why not let someone drive it and help cover the costs of ownership? Want to be bi-coastal? Transcontinental even? Entirely possible, especially if you read this book and learn from others already living the shareable lifestyle. With the sharing economy you can find ways to realize your dreams right here and right now, using the value of what you already have.

You will reduce your reliance on debt

Debt is often the result of buying more than you can afford. What if you thought you had enough and had all the abundance in the world at your fingertips? Well the good news is, you do. With open education and the ability to earn money from your idle time and space - your mortgage, car, and tuition payment might just disappear or be covered by leading a Shareable Life.

You will develop more trust in strangers

None of the co-authors of this book would have thought they'd be lending out their couches to international guests, handing over the keys to their cars, or crowdfunding this book. Now we joke that strangers are simply "friends we haven't met yet."

Throughout the how-to guides in this book, you'll learn various tips on vetting people with ratings, reviews, and digital reputation to create positive sharing experiences.

Join us on a journey through the sharing economy and learn tips and tricks that will change your life for the better.

In this book, we'll show you how to:

► Live rent free

► Pay for your car

► Always have a new outfit

► Make money in your spare time

► Travel the world on the cheap

► Live and work from anywhere

You'll also be charmed by the stories of people we've run across who are participating in the sharing economy - and discover firsthand how you can apply their experiences to your lifestyle.

PART TWO:
Learn How to Share

A Definition For the Sharing Economy

When the three of us co-authors got together, we had many lively discussions about what the sharing economy actually is. We needed a definition in order to decide what to cover in this book and what to omit.

In order to be considered part of the sharing economy, the services in this book have to include the following sharing economy components:

- ▶ Underutilized resource
- ▶ Peer-to-peer exchange
- ▶ Ability to save and/or make money

We decided that the power of the sharing economy is in the peer-to-peer connections people make using stuff, time, space or skills as the bridge for that connection.

In the past, people purchased goods or rented from established companies, but now neighbors, friends, friends-of friends, and perfect strangers can do business with each other.

Today, anyone can be a sharing economy entrepreneur and go into business for themselves - virtually overnight.

This represents a movement toward people helping people frequently referred to as peer-to-peer where everyone can be both a provider and a participant. And this isn't just limited to people trans-acting differently - the sharing economy doesn't always require money.

From gifting to borrowing, swapping, buying, selling, renting, and paying it forward there are many different ways that people share.

WHAT IS THE Sharing Economy?

The Sharing Economy includes:

1. An underutilized resource
2. A peer-to-peer exchange

Resulting in:

The ability for people to save and/or make money

Supported by:

Trust created via digital networks

How to Read this Book

Throughout the following how-to guides, you'll see the icons below, which will help you understand what type of sharing components are involved as well as the monetary benefits. In addition, there are icons that illustrate the type of exchange, including buy, sell, rent, pay it forward, gift, borrow, and swap.

Type of Exchange	Sharing Components
Buy	Underutilized Resource
Sell	Peer to peer
Rent	Save money
Pay it forward	Make money
Gift	
Borrow	
Swap	

Part Three:
Shareable Guides

Shareable Stuff

"The relationship between physical products, individual ownership, and self-identity is undergoing a profound evolution. In other words, we want not the stuff, but the needs or experiences it fulfills."

-Rachel Botsman
Author of What's Mine is Yours

STUFF

DRILL OWNERSHIP
$1,000/hr

The average electric drill only gets used for 13 minutes in its entire life. That brings the cost of drill ownership up to about $1000 per hour.

1/8

One in eight women admit to regularly buying dress they wear ONCE.

Techshop members have used their facilities to design and build everything from jetpacks to satellites.

THIS
V E R Y

graphic was crowd sourced and created for less than $150

ARTISTS RAISED OVER
$1 Billion+

KICK STARTER

Independent artists and visionaries have raised over a quarter of a billion dollars using Kickstarter.

Over 2 BILLION SQUARE FEET OF PUBLIC STORAGE facilities are packed full of all of our unused or rarely used Stuff. That's enough stuff space to completely cover the city of San Francisco twice. And that's just what we put in storage. Imagine all the stuff in your garage and closets!

FREECYCLE has over 9 MILLION MEMBERS in over 85 COUNTRIES. There are over 5,000 LOCAL GROUPS. They save over 600 TONS of stuff from landfills every day.

stuff COSTS

People Like to Share Stuff with People they Live Near

The ever-popular, original source for people to sell, gift, and trade goods and services online is Craigslist. Since 1996, everything under the sun has been on offer, from appliances to ride shares to free furniture. Whatever you're interested in, it can be found or requested there.

Eventually people started using Craigslist in novel ways, like bartering goods, requesting job shares, exchanging specialized goods and services, and even trading urban gardening land. People wanted to share time, objects, resources, and space, and they wanted to reach out to people who lived nearby to do it.

While knocking on a neighbor's door to borrow a cup of sugar doesn't seem as natural as 1950's films make it out to be, 24% of people do borrow something from a neighbor at least once a year, according to a 2011 Harris Interaction study. This suggests that people like to share with those they have relationships with or are in close proximity to.

Reviews Help People Share with People Online

We've seen the meteoric rise of Ebay which enables individuals to sell products online to the general public. Before the mid-'90s, though, the idea of getting a box shipped directly to your home from someone you didn't know and had never met, was more than a little nerve-racking. What if the item wasn't what was described, or was broken, or never arrived? To address these problems, Ebay was the first to create seller ratings, which gave buyers peace of mind and awarded sellers an online badge of trust.

Seller ratings are similar to the reviews used on many sharing economy websites, where people rate a transaction or write a quick blurb regarding their experience. These reviews get associated with profiles of real people that contain social network information like name, photo, and some personal details. These profiles and reviews give others a public context for online trust and reputation.

What Are People Sharing?

Low-cost materials like books, games, movies, and the like are typically not shared locally, but are often swapped outright through websites like swap.com. But when the object of desire is expensive and/or will only be used for a short time or at a special event, then it becomes more convenient, practical, and economical to borrow or rent rather than purchase.

Items like esoteric sports gear, recreational vehicles, and specialized gardening equipment are currently being shared by strangers through online services. And in addition to saving or making money, people doing this have the opportunity to meet others with a common interest.

Ron Williams, the founder of online swapping service Snap-Goods, explains, "Strangers are willing to share, borrow, and rent goods which they can extract immediate value from, such as digital cameras, lab equipment, or tools needed for a short period of time."

In addition to SnapGoods, Ron is building Simplist (simpli.st), a platform showing which users within a network have recently been interested in a particular item or subject area. He believes this information is vital to any goods-sharing service. In the future Simplist will be able to search the people in your social networks to find those with common interests and recent interactions on certain topics. This will help you identify people who have what you need or might be interested in working with you on projects.

Neighborhoods Are Built on Sharing

Sharing stuff works best when people live near each other and have common interests, friends, groups, or workplaces in common. In a NeighborGoods study, 85% of respondents said they wanted to share with people they know. So NeighborGoods is in the process of creating a system by which people can share within their self-identified groups.

Group types where sharing can happen organically:

- ► Neighborhood
- ► Workplace
- ► Church
- ► Gym
- ► Condo association / apartment building
- ► Park / athletic teams
- ► Shared interests (cooking, running, photography, books)

The Costs of Not Sharing

Over 2 billion square feet of public storage facilities in the U.S. are packed full of our unused or rarely used stuff. That's enough to completely cover the entire 49-square-mile city of San

Francisco twice over. We spend 22 billion dollars annually on storage, which is about $70 for every man, woman, and child in America, far outstripping the average family's movie budget. Note that one household in ten has a storage unit. And all this is just what we put in storage. Imagine all the stuff in your garages and closets!

The average electric drill only gets used for 13 minutes in its entire life. That brings the cost of drill ownership up to, oh, about $1,000 per hour!

One in eight women admit to regularly buying dresses they wear once, which kinda begs the question: How's that working for you?

The Benefits of Sharing

Sharing stuff is an easy way to get your feet wet in the sharing economy. You can use websites to get and give away free stuff, clear out your garage, and swap books, CDs, DVDs, and old electronics. In this chapter, we'll also show you how to be stylish without spending another dollar by participating in clothing swaps, teach you how to get free furniture on Craigslist, and how to take your unused stuff and "pay-it-forward" to friends and others who need what you have.

A Case for Being Neighborly

By Gabriel Stempinski

I hate to clean house but I love living in a clean place. So I employ a housekeeper who makes sure the place is ship-shape. I live in one of four lofts on the top floor of a building in San Francisco. Each of my three neighbors has a comparably-sized loft and they all also employ housekeepers. Think about how inefficient it is for four different housekeepers to clean four identical lofts on the same floor of the same building? Think about how much combined travel time is wasted for all those housekeepers? Think about how much wasted setup time, travel time, cleaning equipment, and supplies.

So far we've talked about wasting consumable goods and services, but what about equipment? Let's take my mom's lawnmower as an example. My mom lives in suburbia in Southern California and has a small lawn of about 2,000 square feet. It takes about a half hour to mow the lawn and even in peak growing season it doesn't need mowing more than once a week. That means the mower is in operation less than 20 hours a year. At that rate the mower is less likely to wear out and more likely to rust out or be replaced by a spiffy new model bought in the spring with a tax refund. If she keeps the mower for five years it's been used well south of only a hundred hours. Is this a good bang for her yard care buck?

To make the situation worse the companies that manufacture your stuff know the above usage trends and often utilize a concept called "engineered failure" when designing their goods. Sometimes this is affectionately known as "planned obsolescence." In essence they give their products an expected lifespan. After all, it's bad for business if your widget never breaks, rusts, wears out, or goes on the fritz and hence never needs to be replaced. Luckily for us they also provide manufacturers' warranties on said widgets, albeit only for a limited time.

Let's go back to the lawnmower example. My mom shares her cul-de-sac with six other houses, so why not just have a neighborhood lawnmower that everyone can use? That lawnmower would be in regular operation and could wear out or break down well within the manufacturer's warranty period, which would either get them a brand new lawnmower or free repairs.

Seems so easy, right? Then why aren't we all sharing like this? One of the biggest reasons is the convenience factor, sometimes expressed as "I want to mow my lawn when I feel like it, and not have to wait for my neighbor to finish." Think about the last time you went out to mow the lawn. How many of your neighbors were also out there mowing their lawns right then? And even if your neighbor Mark was out there mowing away, might you be willing to wait a few minutes until he was done, and then borrow the mower?

Here's what I'm getting at. Ownership that creates "convenience" is mostly a myth. So much of your "stuff" is so rarely used that you'd hardly notice that it had been used or was not even there. It's access that creates convenience. If my mom had the lawnmower and her neighbor had the weed whacker and another neighbor had the tiller and another had a mulcher and so on, and they all agreed to share their equipment, then each of them would have access to far more cool lawn gear than any single one of their garages could hold. Not to mention the goodwill built up, the conversations over the back fence, and perhaps the drinks or dinners shared after the work was done, all from being in community with your neighbors.

"Been Sleeping on The Floor for a Year" A Craiglist Story

by Chelsea Rustrum

After I purchased a new California King mattress on Craigslist, I decided to just give away the old mattress via the free section of Craigslist. Within an hour, I had a request from a local college student wanting to come by and pick it up that evening. I felt a strange wave of accomplishment even though nothing had happened yet. When he arrived in a 1997 Honda Civic, I was dumbfounded as to how he was going to transport the full size mattress.

"No big deal!" he said. "I can strap it to my roof."

So I helped my new Craigslist friend carry the mattress outside. With little more than gritty determination and weak twine, we somehow got the thing relatively secured on the top of his car. Before pulling away he waved to thank me. And then came the big shocker, "I've been sleeping on the floor for more than a year, so this will be so nice. Thank you!"

I'll never forget that day – he'd now be able to sleep better and I got my old mattress hauled away for free. We each had won, in ways both tangible and intangible.

Getting something free requires someone else's time, thought, energy, and value. So while these tools are available to everyone, think about obtaining something free as a mutual exchange. Whether you accept their gift, swap with another, or pay it forward in the future, both parties will benefit from the exchange.

How to Get a Free Couch (or Anything Else) on Craigslist

Type of Exchange	Sharing Components
Pay it forward	Underutilized Resource
Gift	Peer to peer
	Save money

If you need a couch, an end table, or a one-of-a-kind objet d'art to finish off the stunning ambiance of your pad, look no further than the sharing economy. In fact, look no further than Craigslist! People are constantly redecorating, replacing furniture, cleaning out garages, etc., and then posting their newly-orphaned items online for you to claim. Most people don't realize that Craigslist has an entire sub-section dedicated to "free" stuff in the "for sale" section.

STEP 1: Head over to Craigslist.org

Most major cities in the U.S. have a pretty active Craigslist with extensive listings for housing, jobs, services, personals, discussions, etc. They also list things for sale by category, and provide "free" and "wanted" listings. If you can't find what you're looking for on Craigslist follow the next how-to guide and look instead on Freecycle.

STEP 2: Find the Free Stuff

In the "for sale" section there is a category called "free". Browse this section and try adding a search string like "couch" to find what you're looking for. You can also search by district and whether the item has an accompanying photo. Note that the items will be listed in chronological order, latest postings being shown first. If you're looking for a specific item, best to check the site regularly so you can respond quickly.

STEP 3: Ask for the Item

Once you've found your item, respond as soon as possible. Craigslist provides an anonymous email address to respond to the ad. Whether you communicate by phone or email, make sure you cover the relevant details:

- ▶ Who you are
- ▶ Why you want their free couch
- ▶ When you can come pick it up
- ▶ If you will need help moving the item
- ▶ All your contact information

STEP 4: Pick It Up

Everyone is busy, so be considerate of people's time. Call, email, and show up when you say you will.

Things you Should Know:

- ► Inspect before taking – make sure you reeeally want this item!
- ► Rips and stains can be remedied with a couch cover
- ► What's most important - shape, size, color, style, comfort, etc.?
- ► Bring a friend to provide enough muscle to cart the thing away

STEP 5: Follow Up

If you scored a free couch, send the donor a follow up email message or text. Better yet, throw in a photo of the couch tastefully situated in your living room.

Insider Tips for Using Craigslist:

Spot a Flake

If someone is inconsistent in their interactions with you, that's your first clue that they might flake on you. If possible, get on the phone with them as soon as you can to verify all the details and set up a time to meet. Be direct, enthusiastic, and specific in your communications to reassure the other person that you're serious as well.

Get the Item You Want

If you have an iPhone, iPad, or an Android, download the cPlus+ app on your phone to turn Craigslist into a multi-dimensional experience. This allows you to browse pictures and descriptions at the same time, and to set alerts when your items become available. The app costs $1.99 and is well worth it if you're going to be using Craigslist on a regular basis.

Be Safe

Always trust your gut. Also try to bring someone along to pick stuff up, or at least tell a friend what you're doing, when you're leaving, when you're coming back, and where you're going. Never (ever) wire money to anyone for any reason as there is no way to get it back. This is probably the #1 Craigslist scam.

Negotiate the Price

If you're buying an item, it's important to note that there is somewhat of a haggling culture on Craigslist.

So, to negotiate well:

► Look for a seller who is in a hurry (perhaps they're relocating)

► Provide evidence that you can get it cheaper elsewhere

► Offer 20% below the maximum that you're willing to pay (this gives you negotiating room)

In summary, Craigslist is a mecca of local information where you can find events, merchandise, roommates, happenings, services, jobs, rides, people, gigs, etc. If you're an entrepreneur, a small business, or someone who provides services to others, Craigslist is a brilliant, high-traffic resource for getting your name out there.

P.S. Other ways to get a free couch: post a request on Facebook or Twitter, and show up after yard sales with a truck — oftentimes there are items left on the curb with a "free" sign. Happy hunting!

HOW TO SCORE FREE STUFF ON FREECYCLE

Type of Exchange	Sharing Components
PAY IT FORWARD	UNDERUTILIZED RESOURCE
GIFT	PEER TO PEER
	SAVE MONEY

Early web phenomenon Freecycle started out in 2003 as an email list between founder Deron Beal and 40 of his local friends. At the time he was working at a nonprofit (RISE), providing recycling services for downtown businesses in Tucson, Arizona. Many of the employees couldn't bear to see perfectly good furniture and electronics being thrown away, so they started driving the goods around town to see if other nonprofits could use them. This inspired the email list, which allowed anyone to give and get items, which later morphed into Freecycle as it's known today.

Still fairly low-tech, Freecycle uses email list groups for communication and is now a nonprofit itself, active in more than 85 countries with more than 8 million members. There are over 5,000 local groups changing the world "one gift at a time", as they like to say. And get this: Freecycle saves a whopping 600 tons of stuff from landfills every day.

You can get everything from baby clothes to hot tubs, love-seats to espresso machines, and pillars to posts on Freecycle. The highest value items are typically the larger ones that are more difficult to move, like couches, desks, refrigerators, and the like. But you can also find random supplies, firewood, fish tanks, shoes, office supplies, and even art on Freecycle.

HOW TO JOIN FREECYCLE

STEP 1: Find Local Groups

Login to Freecycle.org or try finder.trashnothing.com, which overlays all of the Freecycle and other similar groups on a map. You can search by city or zip code, but you will get more hits by city.

STEP 2: Sign Up

You never know what neighboring areas might have to offer, so it's worth it to consider joining all groups within, say, ten miles. There could be some really cool stuff just around the corner.

Most of the groups are set up to use Yahoo Groups for their communications. You can browse Freecycle groups here: groups.yahoo.com, and search for "Freecycle [your city, state]." You'll get basic information on the size and location of the groups. To join any of them, click on "Join This Group!"

You will need to get a free Yahoo email account to join Freecycle – this can be done at mail.yahoo.com. Note that you can choose to have your Freecycle messages sent to any of your email addresses – you don't necessarily need to have them come through your Yahoo email account.

Rules and Guidelines will be sent to you. Also, some groups will ask questions in the body of these first emails that you must respond to in order to join. So make sure you r-e-a-d every last w-o-r-d. 'Nuff said.

Once you've responded as necessary, it could take up to 24 hours to be accepted into the group. Just be aware that the moderator is a real human being, with a life, so be patient.

STEP 3: Set Up Your Email

Once you're accepted as a member, you can choose to receive notifications either in a combined daily digest (you'll get one email daily) or as individual offers (one email for every offer). Note that individual emails can be overwhelming for most people, as some groups can post 100 messages per day. That said, being quick to respond to offers will up your chances significantly in being the chosen recipient. Also note that when you respond to an email only that person will see your reply, so from then on you two carry on a "private" conversation.

Tip: You can set up email filters for certain keywords like: "baby" or "bicycle" or "Balderdash" and then have all other emails skip your inbox. This way you will only receive direct postings that reference those keywords, but you can later view all the messages at your leisure.

STEP 4: How the List Works

Every email subject line will begin with one of these four words:

OFFER – Someone is giving away this item

TAKEN – This item has been taken and is an update to an OFFER ad

WANTED – Someone is requesting this item

RECEIVED – This item was received and is an update to a WANTED ad

If you're looking for a couch, you can post an ad by sending an email to [yourgroupname]@yahoogroups.com with "WANTED: Large Brown or Beige Couch" in the subject line.

Tip: Since attachments are not allowed in Yahoo Groups, you'll need to upload a photo of the item you're offering or paste it into the email itself.

Tip: If you have an iPhone, get the MyFreeStuff app to take photos and post offers more easily on the go.

Tip: Download browser plugins to make using FreeCycle easier. In particular, the Freecycle Member Plug-In helps you create properly formatted messages:

Chrome – Freecycle Searcher

Internet Explorer – Freecycle Member Plug-In

Mozilla – Freecycle Member Plug-In

HOW TO GIVE AWAY FREE STUFF USING FREECYCLE

STEP 1: Create an OFFER

Send an email to [yourgroupname]@yahoogroups.com with OFFER as the first word in the subject line followed by a short, succinct description of the item.

In the body of the email, include:

▶ Name – what is the item?

▶ Details – make, model, color, size, etc.

▶ Condition – be honest! (make sure you mention any flaws)

▶ Availability – times item can be picked up

▶ Location – your city/neighborhood

Tip: If you have the time, take a photo of the item and post it on photobucket.com and then paste the link into the email body. The best listings have photos, but this is not a requirement.

Tip: When considering what to OFFER, realize that what you think is useless, broken, or just plain weird might be someone else's treasure. Also consider all the artists out there who use "found materials" for their works!

STEP 2: Decide Who Gets It

You don't have to give your item to the first person who responds. You can wait 24 hours to see who is the best fit. Anyway, that's more fair, considering not everyone is hovering over their computer 24/7.

You can choose the receiver based on:

▶ How much you liked their message

▶ Who you think will get the most benefit from it

▶ Their proximity to you

▶ If you already know them, etc.

▶ Any other reason (it's up to you!)

Tip: When someone takes the time to write a detailed email, they are more likely to follow through and pick up the item as discussed. However, there is a fine line between "providing detail and/or personality" and the dreaded "TMI" (too much information). Be mindful of everyone's time and energy.

STEP 3: Arrange a Pickup Time

If you've included your available times in the original description, this should cut down on the back-and-forth communications. Arrange a time when you'll be home anyway and give the recipient your phone number in case they get lost or end up running late.

STEP 4: Repost the Item as TAKEN

Once the item has been picked up, update the status of the transaction.

To do this, simply hit Reply to your original posting email, delete the "RE: ", replace the word "OFFER" with "TAKEN", and hit Send. This will alert the community that the item is no longer available.

HOW TO GET FREE STUFF USING FREECYCLE

STEP 1: Find Something You Want

Once you've gotten your email settings working properly, the only things that will show up in your inbox will be items that are relevant to you. You can get a daily digest or an email for every single posting. Now let's see if there's a unicycle out there for your weekend clown gig.

STEP 2: Respond to the OFFER

The "early bird" cliche rings true on Freecycle. Many people are just looking to de-clutter, so the first person who sends them a direct, friendly communication is often the one who gets "the worm" or whatever.

Note that you can also post a WANTED request. If you acquire something this way, be sure to post a RECEIVED follow up message.

When you request an item, be sure to include:

- ► Who you are
- ► Why you want the item
- ► What you'll do with it
- ► Thank them for giving the item away

- ► Tell them when you can pick it up
- ► Include a contact phone number

Tip: Use proper grammar and make sure to spell check your request.

Tip: The ideal timeframe for picking up an item is usually within three days, but this can be negotiated.

STEP 3: Ask Follow Up Questions

Once your request is accepted, get any follow up questions answered quickly to make sure the item is a fit. If you determine that it's not right for you, let the poster know as soon as possible so they can OFFER it to someone else.

STEP 4: Be Courteous

If you flake out on picking up an item, you're not doing your Freecycle community any favors and you may get labeled as a no-show or even banned, depending on the rules of the group. If an emergency comes up, give as much advance notice as possible.

Tip: If you arrive and the item is not as described, you can politely decline and ask that they give it to someone else. You are under no obligation.

Tip: When someone gives you something, acknowledge them with a heartfelt thank you. They could have sold the item, but instead took the time to post it and meet up with you, so be a gracious receiver. You might consider making their day by sending them an actual handwritten thank you note.

Freecycle Summary

Communities like Freecycle thrive on giving, so take a moment to think about anything you're not using that another Freecycler might benefit from. If you're a part of the 10% of American households that has a storage unit, consider whether those possessions are worth the money you pay out month after month, year after year. There are people who could greatly benefit from what you have locked away.

Freecycle is a wonderful way to clear out that storage unit, or your garage, or even de-clutter your home. You can start small – gift that juicer you haven't used in a decade, or offer up those books you'll never read again. You'll be glad you did, and so will others.

Additional Freecycle Tips and Tricks:

- ► There is no trading on Freecycle –it's giving and receiving only

- ► Bartering has its own set of rules and government regulations, so do not attempt to trade or barter items as that will get you banned

- ► Arrange a pickup and give the item to one person, not a "whoever gets to my driveway first, gets it" (AKA "wildcatting" or "cattle-calling")

- ► Only provide a phone number to the person you're giving the item to or receiving it from – don't post phone numbers in WANTED or OFFER ads, or you'll be inundated with calls

- ► It's a violation to sell items acquired through Freecycle

- ► When you join, try to offer something first before making requests – it's good etiquette and gets you in the community spirit

- ► Don't be too quick to jump on something just because it's free – consider the cost of gas and your time in picking the item up

- ► If someone seems dodgy in their posting or correspondence, trust your gut – there are no safety or verification measures on Freecycle

- ► Take a friend or family member along with you to pick items up

Wondering How Well Freecycle Works?

To give you an idea, there is a family that relocated from overseas into a new, empty house. They used Freecycle, yard sales, and thrift stores to furnish their entire house for under $200! Read more about how they did it on the "Slow This Ride Down" blog:

Another Option for Requesting & Gifting Free Stuff

As an alternative to Freecycle, try yerdle.com, a new colorful, easy to use mobile app and website for gifting stuff that you don't want or need anymore. You can also request free items that are located across the country, paying only for shipping and handling.

How to Get a Shareable Prom Dress

Type of Exchange	Sharing Components
Rent	Underutilized Resource
Swap	Peer to peer
Pay it forward	Save money
Gift	

Prom is a rite of passage, a night where every girl dreams of looking her best and feeling like a princess. However, the cost of a prom dress can make even a princess feel like a pauper. But instead of having to buy her entire ensemble and dropping hundreds or possibly thousands of dollars, a girl can now rent her perfect dress from a service online. There is nothing revolutionary about renting a dress, as tuxedo rentals have always been an option for guys. The sharing economy gives women the ability to wear special occasion dresses without having to buy them. For example, at renttherunway.com, a free membership service, dresses that retail for $1,200 can be rented for $80 or less.

How to Rent a Designer Dress (or Two)

There's a good FAQ section on the renttherunway.com website that will answer most of your questions. Note that there are several options. You can get a free second size with each order as a backup. You can rent your dresses for either a four-day or eight-day period. If the dresses don't fit, you don't pay (less the cost of shipping). As you check out, you'll be given options for accessories to rent and beauty items to purchase. You pay a modest fee to ship the rented dress to your home, but return shipping is always free. And if you plan on renting dresses frequently, join the Pro progam, which has an annual fee, but will cover the cost of unlimited shipping, dress insurance on every order, and qualify you for a free dress rental on your birthday every year.

If you invite friends and they choose to rent something, they get a $20 discount toward their first purchase and you get $20 bucks for future rentals as well. Money in the bank!

Need a Designer Handbag?

There is a scene in the Sex and the City movie where Carrie Bradshaw is interviewing an applicant who can't afford her apartment, but wears a designer handbag that costs over $1,000. When Carrie inquires, the girl talks about renting her purse on the website, bagborroworsteal.com. You can too, but note that these bags aren't cheap. Even if you're only renting them, they can total up to a car payment real quick.

Can't Afford to Rent a Dress?

You can always try to borrow one from a friend. Or you can check Craigslist.org under "clothes+acc" and search for "dresses".

Or try a "wanted" ad under the "for sale" section, but note that you'll be lumped in with all other items for sale. You can also join a local Freecycle group and put your WANTED request out there. And finally, you can consider clothing swaps. Use swapping websites like i-ella.com, swapstyle.com, or attend a local clothing swap. Also check out, thredup.com where you can buy previously used dresses.

Want to Donate Your Old Dress?

That's the sharing spirit!

You can do so through princessproject.org, which works with with volunteers and donors to provide dresses to high school girls who cannot otherwise afford them.

The Good News

Clothes don't have to be expensive – not even for the prom! There is a whole world of dresses out there that you can rent, borrow, or swap. With the sharing economy you can always look fabulous, wearing anything from unique to designer. Just start using these resources to take control of your look and your wardrobe. Your budget will be glad you did.

How to Swap Your Clothes and Always Have a New Outfit

Type of Exchange	Sharing Components
Swap	Underutilized Resource
Barter	Peer to Peer
Pay it forward	Save money
Gift	

Swapping is a very efficient and fun way to rid yourself of excess "stuff". Clothes are wonderful to share because they are something that we all buy, outgrow, or otherwise feel disassociated with over time. At the moment, clothing swaps are primarily run by women for women's clothing, but you could easily change that by setting one up for young men or children in your hometown.

Americans spend 3.8% of their annual income on clothes, totaling $1,800-2,000 per year on average. Even more startling,

Americans throw out or donate an average of 68 pounds of clothing per year. Obviously, fashion tastes and requirements change, but that is an absurd amount of waste and lost value. However, swapping clothes can help refresh a wardrobe, reduce disposal and consumption, and save you a heck of a lot of cash. Plus, what's sexier? A generic tee-shirt from American Apparel or a unique outfit you put together where each item has it's own story? Used clothing not only saves the environment and your pocketbook, it makes it easier to create your own look and personal fashion statements.

And don't think recycled clothing is limited to hipsters, hippies, and bargain-basement-budgeteers. If you love high-quality designer clothing, there's a fashion swap in your future as well.

STEP 1: Search for Swaps

Look on Meetup.com

Meetup is your best bet for dipping your foot in the water. With over 80 active cities and more than 12,000 members, you can surely find a local swap that suits your tastes when you head over to clothesswap.meetup.com and search by zip code. Join any groups that look interesting.

Do a Google Search

Half the battle is knowing that clothing swaps exist. So you can search for "clothing swap [your city]" to see the various meetup.com groups, informal swap groups, as well as local recycled clothing stores. You might consider using the latter to drop off as consignment items any leftover clothes that weren't taken at the swap itself.

STEP 2: RSVP for a Swap

First things first – secure your spot! Clothing swaps are getting really popular, so you'll need to RSVP early to get on the list. Some swaps charge a fee to cover the cost of the space and any food, but most are free and put on by community members who are passionate about trading clothes.

When you RSVP, good swapping etiquette suggests providing details on:

- ► Articles you're bringing (i.e. dresses, pants, tops, shoes, etc.)
- ► Sizes of the articles
- ► Your age (to gauge clothing styles)
- ► If you're bringing any guests
- ► If you're bringing food or drink to share

STEP 3: Prepare for the Swap

Find 8-10 swappable clothing items. You'll want to bring lightly-worn or like-new clothes. Leave behind anything that's substandard. A good rule is: would you be proud to lend the article to a friend? You should wash the items and fold them or iron (if necessary). If you have nice dresses, you might want to bring them on hangers.

Swappable:

- ► New or gently used
- ► No rips, tears, stains, or broken zippers
- ► Clean, bright, and freshly laundered
- ► Modern or in-fashion style
- ► Clothing including: blouses, skirts, dresses, pants, shoes, and accessories

Not Swappable:

- ► Swimwear
- ► Lingerie
- ► Clothing that's been worn out

STEP 4: Attend the Swap

Now, for the fun part – attend the swap and be open to meeting new people, having a good time, and acquiring a new wardrobe.

Be on Time

This might sound like a no-brainer, but if you're late – you just might miss the actual swap. The format of the swap can vary – attendees might be given viewing numbers or a bell might be rung with everyone running amuck. As crazy as that sounds, however, most clothing swaps do operate with varying degrees of organization. So, like many things in life, being on time is your first key to success.

Be Polite

Don't trip over people or push and shove to get to the clothes first – there will be plenty to go around. Remember, it's a clothing swap, not a rugby scrum.

Be Social

Try stuff on, ask for advice from others, and suggest or share articles you think might look great on someone else.

Follow the Rules

All clothing swaps have rules that will usually be outlined by the host at the beginning. So it's important to pay attention to understand how the swap works, how long it will go, and what will be done with any unclaimed articles, which are often donated to charity.

Other Virtual Clothing Swap Options:

Swapstyle.com

This is an online swap site over 4 million items. Members post photos of their clothing items and accessories and associate each item with a dollar value. These are one-to-one exchanges, so if you want to swap with someone, you need to have enough "value" on offer to close the deal. Swapstyle.com is free to use.

I-ella.com

With i-ella.com, you can buy, sell, borrow, or swap designer clothing and handbags.

Clothing swaps are fun, social, economical, and enable you to always have a stylish wardrobe. With swaps you can find unique clothing and accessories that you'd never see anywhere else. You don't have to be rich to be trendy – you just need to know about swapping.

How to "Pay it Forward" Using Facebook

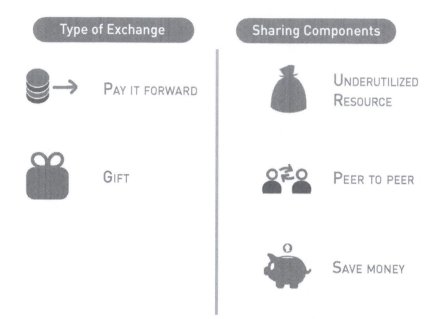

Type of Exchange	Sharing Components
Pay it forward	Underutilized Resource
Gift	Peer to peer
	Save money

This term was made popular by the movie of the same name that debuted in the year 2000. "Pay it forward" means giving something away or doing something for someone else without any expectation of getting anything in return. Instead, the idea is that if you do nice things for people, they might catch on and do the same for others, thus creating a never-ending cascade of giving.

As we have seen in this chapter, stuff can be a burden, so you can unburden yourself through sharing. But sharing stuff doesn't require you to join a new network. You can share with people you already know and care about using a Facebook photo album, in the same way you share vacations, celebrations, and other important events in your life.

STEP 1: Take Photos

Use your cell phone, smart phone, or digital camera to take pictures of each item you want to give away. This will make the images easy to upload.

STEP 2: Create an Album

Log on to Facebook. From your home page, profile, or status update form, click on "Photos" then click "Albums", then click "Create New Album". You can name it "Stuff I Am Giving Away" or something equally creative to let people know that you're giving things away, not selling them.

Create an Album Description

You want to tell people what's inside the album. For example, if you're giving away multiple items your description could be "coffee table, baby clothes, a CD player used only for Abba albums, and size 9 women's shoes". This will show up right below the title and above the album photos.

Tag your Local Friends

This will propagate the album on their wall which allows their friends to also see your stuff as well. Don't tag more than ten people in the area and focus on friends who have the most diverse local connections to maximize your exposure.

Tip: Make sure you post the album as "public" on Facebook so you can link to the album by email, on Twitter, or through other social streams.

STEP 3: Post a Link on Craigslist

After waiting a reasonable amount of time, if your local network is not interested in your free stuff, then it's time to invite the general public. If you want to give your stuff away in record time, don't skip this step.

Post your album to your local Craigslist by going to the "for sale" section on the homepage and click on the "free" category. From there, click on the "[post]" link in the upper right corner and choose the "free stuff" category. Then post a description and at least one photo of your items, along with a descriptive title. You can also include a link to your public Facebook album.

Other Ways to Share Stuff

The sharing resources that are the most widespread primarily involve donating, swapping, renting, borrowing, or operating on the gift economy mentality of paying it forward. You've been shown how to get a free couch on Craigslist, how to de-clutter using Freecycle, and how to swap clothing with others online and through informal social swaps.

However, sharing small stuff like hand drills and blenders has been problematic unless the barriers to do so are low. At least until now.

Swap Your Stuff Online

Swapping is getting really interesting online. Say you have an iPad you don't use anymore and what you really want is the new iPhone. With the efficiency of the internet, you can arrange a swap to do just that. In fact, there are many places where you can swap goods, electronics, clothes, and valuables:

Yerdle.com – Give and receive items for free using an iPhone or Android app. The catch is, it's a credit based system where you get 250 credits to spend on goods when you join, but if you want to continue to bid on goods, you must earn credits by giving away your own stuff.

Tradeya.com — This is a one-to-one swap where you can offer up your own goods and services (everything from electronics, clothes and coupons to services like web page design can be exchanged). They say it's the "easiest way to get anything without buying it."

Swapdom.com — Currently, most of the goods on Swapdom are clothing and housewares, but you can list anything you want. Swapdom makes swapping efficient by using a matching algorithm that makes sure each person gets exactly what they want.

Listia.com — With 7 million members and millions of auctions, Listia also works on a credit system. You'll get 1,000 credits for signing up and another 500 for listing your first item. You can purchase items with your credits and if you run out, you can buy additional credits to purchase items.

Clothing swaps — As mentioned in an earlier section, sites like i-ella.com and swapstyle.com allow you to swap clothing online. Also, consider checking out threadup.com, which allows you to sell clothing you won't use anymore and buy other peoples gently used garmets.

Rent or Borrow Stuff from People Nearby

You can also rent or borrow items from people who live nearby using:

Neighborgoods.net — Join free and see who else is borrowing or renting stuff in your neighborhood. The site uses peer ratings and reviews to build the trust factor. Members, businesses, clubs, and organizations can create public and private groups. The site can be a bit difficult to navigate, but it's one of the first and most neighborhood-specific sharing services we've seen. Currently the coverage is best only in the major cities.

Peerby.com — You can submit a request to borrow anything and Peerby will ping your neighbors to see if they can help you out. Need an ice chest and tent for an upcoming camping trip? Try Peerby.

Use Your Local Tool Lending Library

Tool libraries are set up for locals to have a pooled resource for finding and using tools for things like fixing your car or completing home improvement projects. To find a tool library near you do a Google search for "tool library" in your city.

Participate in a Local Gift Market

An entire gift market can be set up with free stuff for everyone. These help to both build community and keep stuff out of landfills. You can bring stuff to give, but that's not required. Bartering and trading are not allowed – only giving! These markets have started popping up in urban areas. For information on free markets and how to start one in your city, check out the one started in Baltimore: freestorebaltimore.org.

Sharing is for Everyone

If you take one thing away from this chapter, remember that sharing is for everyone! Next time you need something, consider borrowing, renting, swapping, or trying to get it free. From a constantly updated wardrobe to a living room with all the right touches, you don't need to be a millionaire to live like one. And on the flip side, instead of throwing away possessions you no longer want – gift them to someone who can give them a good home.

Shareable Food

"We are already producing enough food to feed the world. We already have technology in place that allows us to produce more than we can find a market for."

-Jeremy Rifkin
Author of The Third Industrial Revolution

Americans throw away just over

40% of their food every year (most of which is produce)

$2,275

>40%
EVERY YEAR

The average family of 4 throws away an equivalent of $2,275 worth of food every year.

440 Mlbs
OF FOOD WASTE
EVERY DAY

If you piled it all together our daily food waste would be about the same size as 2.5 aircraft carriers or just enough to completely fill the Rosebowl and that's just each DAY.

= $$$

You can grow $700 worth of produce on just 100 sqft of (roughly the size of a small bedroom)
Even a modest garden can drastically reduce your food bills.

In cities like San Francisco, Los Angeles, Portland, Seattle, Chicago, Atlanta (and MANY others), it is perfectly legal to keep a small number of egg laying chickens on your property provided they have a proper enclosure.

Food COSTS

Access to Good Food

Good food is getting scarcer by the day. With all the current technology and infrastructure in the developed world, you'd think getting wholesome and fresh food to our populations would be easy. However, in many ways we seem to be worse off than we were 50 years ago.

For example, in order to keep up with America's growing population we've shifted towards industrial farming and highly processed food that will "keep" for a long period of time (twinkies, anyone?). The amount of locally grown food available in our grocery stores is shrinking to the point that we now consider "local food" to be luxury items. Due to this shift in agricultural and marketing practices we get foods laden with preservatives, chemicals, salt, and artificial sweeteners. Even worse, the food has been stripped of much of it's essential nutrition, which leads to increasing incidences of obesity, diabetes, cancer, hypertension, and heart disease.

This particularly strikes hard at the poor and lower middle class for whom "real foods" are not even available in many neighborhoods, leading these areas to be labeled "food deserts". "Real foods" are those items that aren't over-processed, sprayed with harsh pesticides, or grown with petroleum-based fertilizers.

Access to "real food" is essential for our healthy future and this section will tell you how utilize the sharing economy to feed yourself and your family, shrink your grocery bill, build community, and, most importantly, stay healthy. We'll cover everything from shared meals and experiences to ways you can maximize the distribution of underutilized food in your hometown. We'll also give you ideas for growing produce even if you don't have a yard of your own.

As it turns out, sharing food isn't as simple as sharing experiences. But new laws, such as the Cottage Food Act are being passed in many states to make it easier for individuals to prepare food in their homes and legally share their culinary creations.

How to Share a Meal in Your Home
Eatwith.com / Eatfeastly.com

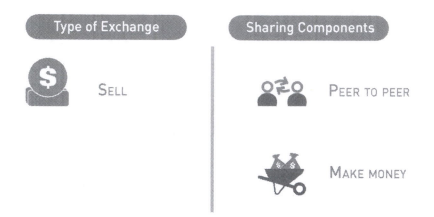

Type of Exchange

$ SELL

Sharing Components

PEER TO PEER

MAKE MONEY

Do you love to host dinners, throw parties, and get people together? If so, you know that hosting can be time consuming, labor intensive, and quite costly. Perhaps you're looking to meet people outside of your inner circle, practice your gourmet cooking skills, or simply want to meet other foodies - meal sharing allows you to do all of this and more!

If you like meeting new people and connecting with your community, shared dining experiences might be for you. Meal sharing services like eatwith.com and eatfeastly.com, help you plan, organize, and fund your event, as well as invite strangers to sit around your table and enjoy your culinary creations.

HOW TO GET STARTED

STEP 1: Join Up (It's Free)

Head to eatwith.com and/or eatfeastly.com to sign up.

With eatfeastly.com, you can directly sign up to "Become a Cook." However, eatwith.com has a review process for choosing new chefs. To begin with, you will have to sign up as a regular member.

To become a meal host on eatwith, you can apply at: (eatwith.com/brand/be-a-host).

STEP 2: Sign up to "Become a Cook" & Post a Meal

Since eatfeastly.com has an immediate sign up process, the rest of the details in this guide will pertain to Feastly.

► Fill in Details About Your Bio

Choose a personable photo of yourself and fill out a description of who you are, your cooking interests, and history as it pertains to food.

► Add Photos of Food, Your Cooking Space, & Dining Area

The photos are what is ultimately going to sell your meal, so don't skip this step. Your photos should tell a story of what people can expect when they come to your home.

Tip: Do a practice run of the meal you'd like to submit. Invite a few friends over, cook the same meal you'll serve your future guests, and take high quality photos of the whole experience. That way, you'll be able to show people what your meal will be like.

▶ Fill in the Event Details, Including the Menu

You'll need to create a custom title, event description, and the menu of courses. This is where you can choose the cuisine type and food categories (such as gluten free, vegan, paleo, etc.).

STEP 3: Wait For Your Submission to be Reviewed

Yep, it's a case of hurry up and wait! Assuming you posted a quality meal with detailed photos, plan to hear from someone soon so that you can host your first meal.

Tip: Be professional and witty in all of your biographical details, your interest in becoming a home cook, and the title of of your meal. Make sure you're doing something that's original, catchy, and will likely be a hit!

How to Create a Free Farm Stand in Your Community

Type of Exchange

Pay it forward

Gift

Sharing Components

Underutilized Resource

Peer to peer

Save money

FreeFarmStand.org and TheFreeFarm.org – Founded in 2008

The Free Farm Stand, located in the Mission district of San Francisco, distributes free food through gifting organic fruits, vegetables, and locally made breads every weekend.

The food is sourced from produce that goes unsold at farmer's markets, and from neighborhood and community gardens, and also from public and private fruit trees. Additionally, they help grow food on donated land. The Free Farm Stand builds community and provides a meeting place for locals on tight budgets. Most learn about the Free Farm Stand by word-of-mouth as there is little to no press and barely enough information online to even deduce the time and place of the weekly event.

On distribution days people start arriving around noon and request a number which will be used to admit groups of ten at a time. Many folks picnic or sit in circles on the grass and talk while they wait their turn. There is no sense that this is any sort of handout or cattle call, but rather a way to connect to the community, get needed food, and foster a sense of belonging.

The founder, and long-time farmer, explains "We want to improve trust and sharing through this gift economy. The idea is, if you give something, the universe will take care of you."

While the Free Farm Stand may sound overly tree-hugger and hippy-dippy to some readers, this is a beautiful example of taking unused food that would likely be wasted otherwise and distributing it to those in need. It's a win-win.

If you're not motivated by the sheer altruism of the idea, think of it this way. Food insecurity drives people to seek public assistance (e.g., food stamps and other forms of welfare) that strain state and local budgets. Community-driven activities like this decrease both food insecurity and public assistance. Just another example of how sharing reduces waste, strengthens communities, and helps relieve already overburdened government budgets.

HOW TO START A FREE FARM STAND IN YOUR COMMUNITY

STEP 1: Get Organized

Find a location and round up a few friends who are willing to help out. When scouting locations stick to open spaces and avoid sidewalks. The key is to be sufficiently visible to make distribution easy but not overly obtrusive as to attract, say, attention from the authorities. Small neighborhood parks are ideal, or even parking lots of local businesses who agree to let you set up there.

Keep in mind there may be local laws requiring permits before setting up a stand. It's probably best to first check with city hall about this.

STEP 2: Collect the Food

You might be surprised to find out there are many sources of free food out there. Go to your local farmers market when everyone is closing up and ask the produce vendors if they have any food to donate. Put together a friendly pitch about your stand and explain what you're trying to do. Tell the vendors you're willing to take anything that isn't selling well or that would spoil before their next market day. You'll be surprised how many vendors will be willing to contribute. Make sure you have crates, boxes, or bags to take away your haul.

If you live in an area where many people have fruit trees in their yards, you can also go door to door and ask them if they'd like to donate excess fruit. For example, when you drive through neighborhoods in Southern California you often see every other house with orange or lemon trees absolutely heavy with fruit. Much of this is likely to go to waste, because how many lemons can one family eat? Many home owners will be happy to give you their extras, even if it's just to avoid the cleanup when the fruit starts falling to the ground.

You can also ask around at local bakeries and neighborhood grocery stores. Unfortunately, the large chain groceries will likely have policies forbidding food donations due to liability concerns, but the locally owned stores may be more amenable to helping you.

STEP 3: Get the Word Out

Set up your distribution schedule and disseminate your information to all the local neighborhood organizations. Call your local Department of Human Services about which community outreach programs may be able to help you spread the word. You might even consider creating a Yelp page to make your stand locatable on the internet. This will establish an indexable address for your listing so that people can find the details online.

STEP 4: Distribute the Food

This is where the rubber meets the road. You want to make sure the food gets evenly distributed but as you're just starting out you won't know how to gauge the demand. You might try pre-packing bags of mixed produce, bread, and whatever else you have, and give one out to each person. If fewer people than expected are showing up, you can add more food into each bag. If more people show up, your marketing campaign has been successful, and you can make adjustments next time.

Tip: Invite other friends and people you know to picnic, play instruments, and hang out nearby. After all nothing draws a crowd like a crowd!

STEP 5: Don't Get Frustrated

In the first few weeks you'll likely be playing it by ear. It takes a while for the news to get out. Worst case scenario is that the few folks who do come will get a whole bunch of free food, which will make them likely to spread the word. Stick with it!

For more details check out the San Francisco Free Farm Stand blog at freefarmstand.org.

HOW TO SET UP AN URBAN FARM FOR SHARING FOOD

Type of Exchange	Sharing Components
PAY IT FORWARD	UNDERUTILIZED RESOURCE
GIFT	PEER TO PEER
	SAVE MONEY

Urban farming is the practice of growing, processing, and distributing food in a city. This food can originate from standard farms, orchards, fish ponds, chicken coops, beehives, etc. Urban farms make fresh vegetables, organic fruits, and other wholesome food products available to local consumers who otherwise would have access only to processed or preserved foods, or would have to pay a premium for higher food transportation costs. Urban farming also provides additional benefits like recreation, education, relaxation, and community building. If you already have an urban farm in your city you can join up and work with the collective in exchange for some of the harvest. Or if you aren't the gardening type you can buy their products at local farmers markets and support the, uh, growing "local food" movement. This way, you'll also get higher-quality and better-tasting farm fresh goods than you would from the chain grocery stores. If you want to start your own urban farm then all you need do is follow these instructions.

HOW TO START A SHARED URBAN FARM

STEP 1: Organize!

Get a group of like-minded folks together and write up a plan for the following:

- ▶ What materials, land, and equipment will you need?
- ▶ How will the membership of the farm be structured?
- ▶ How will tasks and responsibilities be allocated to members?
- ▶ What crops will be grown (hopefully year-round)?
- ▶ What food distribution methods will be utilized?
- ▶ How much product will each member receive?
- ▶ How much product will be donated to local charities? (this is useful in securing the political good will of local government offices or organizations that will donate land)
- ▶ How much product (if any) will be sold at local markets to generate income to support the farm?
- ▶ How will the farm attract new members?
- ▶ What benefits will the farm provide to the community at large? (school groups, outreach, special programs, etc.)

STEP 2: Find Land for Your Farm

This isn't as difficult as you might think. If you can show that you're going to use the farm to benefit the community, many cities or private groups might be willing to allow you to plant on their vacant space. The key is your sales pitch.

Here are some ideas to help sweeten the deal:

- ► Donate a portion of your produce to homeless shelters
- ► Coordinate with the school district to do field trips for children
- ► Show how you intend to beautify otherwise unsightly vacant land
- ► Explain how locally produced "real food" benefits the entire community
- ► Get your neighborhood supervisor, city council person, or other mid-level public officials to help champion your cause

STEP 3: Plan Your Farm

Research Crop Types

It's important to keep the farm producing all year round. Make sure you choose crops for each season so that you always have something growing and something ready for harvest.

Research Crop Yields

Determine which crops will provide the most food per unit space and thus give you the most product for your efforts.

Map Out the Plot

There's a certain joy in planning and designing the layout of your farm. Whether you use graph paper or software like Visio or CAD, make sure your plot layout will allow for easy watering, weeding, and harvesting.

Design for Equipment and Irrigation

Make sure you include space for any equipment usage and storage, and details about how you plan to water your crops. You should have your complete design ready to submit (at least in rough draft) when you're petitioning for land use.

Ask for Assistance

If you want tips on technical issues, reach out to other urban farmers. It's a near guarantee that they'll be willing to give advice, if not actual physical help. You can even email the authors! You'll likely find many people who would love to help you out and/or provide information.

STEP 4: Build the Infrastructure

This is where you'll need to spend some money to get the venture up and running. There's a good chance the soil on your urban plot is poor and not suited for farming, so you'll likely need to buy or get some donated topsoil and a tiller to enrich and break up the soil. If that's not possible at least try to break up the hard stuff by hand and add in compost or other nutrients as available.

Prepare the Soil

There are ways you can save a lot of money on this step if you think ahead. Have your farm members start collecting their food wastes for compost which can be tilled directly into the soil. You can also pick up some inexpensive natural chicken manure to help enrichment. It's worth a call to the agricultural departments of any local colleges and universities. There you may find a grad student or professor who would be willing to come out and do a soil analysis and give you some free advice or at least some "dirt cheap" pointers.

Set Up the Irrigation

Depending on your chosen irrigation method you'll either need to dig trenches and lay pipes for sprinklers or drip lines, or buy hoses for above ground sprinklers. You might be able to get local garden stores or locally owned hardware stores to donate or discount their goods in return for posting up their name at your farm. No harm in asking for outright donations either.

Build a Fence

If there isn't already some sort of fence around your farm now is the time to install one. If you have the money you could put up a chain link fence or build a cheaper wooden post and beam model. Even if you're not farming in a high-traffic area you'll need to protect your plot from critters and local kids who may mistake your farm for a playground.

STEP 5: Plant Your Farm

Follow the instructions on the seed packages or, if you're buying seedlings, from the garden store personnel. You want to maximize yields but you don't want to over-crowd your plants, either. Keep an eye on the weather reports in the first few weeks after planting when your crops are most vulnerable and susceptible to flooding out, drying out, or freezing. Once again there are surely some folks with ultra-green thumbs in your community who have lots of experience with this.

STEP 6: Promote Your Farm

Talk to the community in the area around the farm, display an eye-catching banner on the fence, put together a website, get local kids involved through the schools, etc. There's lots of free labor around and plenty of folks who would be willing to get their hands dirty just for the joy of gardening. You can even set up a request on time - and skill-sharing websites like Time-banks.org to get other people involved and helping out (see Shareable Education).

STEP 7: Maintain Your Farm

Ensure your members are in agreement as to the rotation of tasks. The responsibility for maintaining the farm should be spread out evenly. It shouldn't take more than a few hours per week per person to keep up with all the work to be done, even less if you have a good base of volunteers. You may also want to talk to a local beekeeper to get a hive box put on your plot to help out with the pollination. This also gives you one more item to harvest (i.e. honey), which is especially important these days given all the alarming hive collapses.

STEP 8: Harvest!

If you plant a good variety of crops you should be able to con-stantly keep harvesting something. This way there's a steady supply of fresh produce to all the members and perhaps items to sell at local farmers markets. We're not going to pretend to be master farmers but anyone can do searches on terms like year round gardening vegetable plan" or "vegetable garden annual crop rotation" and get good tips and tricks for their region.

STEP 9: (Most Importantly) Share

Don't forget to benefit the community. Be creative and use some of your harvested goods to support something you believe in. Get people engaged and helping with every step of the planting, weeding, watering, harvesting, distribution, promotion, outreach, and the educational benefits of the farm.

For inspiration, check out: urbanhomestead.org which describes how the Dervaes family grows 7,000 pounds of food annually on 1/10th of an acre utilizing basic farming techniques. They're a great example of how you can supplement your own and your community's food supplies on a small amount of land with just spare-time volunteer support.

OTHER SHAREABLE FOOD SERVICES

Join a Community Supported Agriculture Group (CSA)

A Community Supported Agriculture Group (otherwise known as a CSA) is a club where you agree to buy a share of locally grown produce (typically fruits and vegetables) each week directly from a farmer. Many farmers offer a specific number of "shares" to the public, which makes it easy to eat locally grown food, even when you live in a city. Some CSAs also offer bread, cheese, eggs, flowers, etc.

Most CSAs have a drop-off location in a local neighborhood, which are often at a member's home. The member would then divide the delivery up into individual portions to be picked up by the members. CSAs also have flexibility as some accept food stamps or offer scholarships to those who can't afford to pay. CSA payments make it easier for farmers to plan and pay for their growing season. You can use localharvest.org to find a CSA near you.

Sharing Extra Fruit & Vegetables

There are many fruit trees in public areas, so websites like oaklandtrees.com (in Oakland, CA) provide an online map with 40,000 fruit trees on public property within the city where you can pick fruit free of charge. There is also fallenfruit.org, which generates maps of public spaces and private trees offered to the public in locations all over the world.

Selling & Gifting Leftover Food

Shareyourmeal.net (more widely used in Western Europe) and leftoverswap.com are ways for people sell and gift entrees to people nearby. Since there is such an incredible amount of food wasted every minute, services like these as well as simple solutions at public hubs can help distribute not only residental leftovers, but also the leftovers and soon-to-expire goods generated by local businesses and grocery stores.

Dinners Made by Neighborhood Chefs

With munchery.com, you can buy carefully crafted dinners made by people in your neighborhood, prepared in the comfort of their homes, and delivered to your door. These meals are well-planned and are not mass-produced, so the end result is something unusually fresh, healthy, and scrumptious. And you'd be surprised that most meals are less than $20 per serving, even with delivery.

Meals Made by Locals in Your Kitchen

Kitchensurfing.com is different from meal sharing websites eatwith.com and eatfeastly.com in that the service allows groups of people who want a meal made in their kitchen choose the location, number of guests and cuisine wanted, and then select a menu to be prepared by a specific chef in their home.

Shared Kitchens for Hobbyist Chefs

Shared kitchens are often fully functional commercial grade kitchens, which are professionally permitted and licensed. Hobbyist chefs, small scale catering organizations, food cart vendors, or other interested parties can get access to prepare food in typically larger volumes for sale or service. Shared kitchens are also a great place to practice your cooking skills with professional equipment before making large capital investments. To find a shared kitchen, head to culinaryincubator.com and also look at sffoodlab.com as a good example.

Group Cooking and Meal Trading

Along the same lines of shared kitchens is mamabake.com where a group of people gathers together socially and cooks a number of dinner dishes. Then each person swaps something like a quiche for a lasagna and – voila! – a variety of meals for the week are done, all at once! And you don't need MamaBake to make this happen – just send out an email invitation to some friends and spend two hours cooking per week instead of 6-8!

Most holidays, family traditions, and events revolve around food. And that is for good reason! Food is a connector, a way to build community, and vital to our survival. As you think about Shareable Food, consider how sharing a meal, your leftovers, extra fruit, garden space, and land will help everyone lead healthier, more fulfilling lives.

Shareable Travel

"What is an experience? Something that breaks a polite routine and for a brief period allows us to witness things with the heightened sensitivity afforded to us by novelty, danger, or beauty — and it's on the basis of shared experiences that intimacy is given an opportunity to grow."

-Alain de Botton
Author of The Architecture of Happiness

TRAVEL

Average Vacation VS Sharing Vacation

Bureau of Labor Stats breaks down travel cost as:

44%: Transportation
23%: Food + Beverages
23%: Lodging
10%: Entertainment

Therefore the average vacation:

$704: Transportation
$368: Food + Beverages
$368: Lodging
$160: Entertainment

NYC

$350 — Average cost of hotel

$170 — Airbnb average private home /apartment
(and since you have your own apartment you can make your own food if you want)

$100 — Average Private room

This means, with the **average vacation budget, a family of 3 could buy:**

Off season discount airfare to NYC for 2 days 1 night

Have 1 nice meal

Stay one night in a hotel

Go on 1 tour

ADMIT ONE

Using Vayable, there are hundreds of tours and experiences for under $30 per person

This means using shareable model, on the average vacation budget, a family of three could buy:

Off season discount airfare to NYC for 2 days 1 night

Stay 3 airbnb nights

Have 1 nice meal

Go on 3 shareable tours

ADMIT ONE

for exactly the same price.

Travel COSTS

This section will teach you how to obtain shared accommodations and have shared experiences by using the following services:

Couchsurfing – you don't actually surf with anyone, but you can stay on local peoples' couches all over the world – for free! And if you're not currently traveling, you could host travelers on your own couch, in your spare bedroom, or even let them pitch a tent in your back yard. Couchsurfing does not cost money and is based on the "pay it forward" mentality, in that by hosting travelers you'll inspire them to host other travelers (maybe even you!). The community acts as a social and cultural exchange for people all over the world. At last count, there were over 9 million members, enabling you to find Couchsurfing hosts even in the proverbial Timbuktu.

Airbnb – From your couch to your extra bedroom, Airbnb enables you to host anyone you choose and get paid for it. You can rent out your entire house, an apartment, a bedroom, an RV, or your trusty ol' sailboat "Sloopy." Basically, anywhere someone can sleep can be offered up as a place to stay, at whatever price you set.

HOUSE SWAPPING – There are many services that make it possible to swap your house or condo with someone on the other side of the planet. We'll tell you how right here.

VAYABLE (shareable experiences) – Do you like to do "insider" local activities when you travel? Interested in learning about new fun things to do in the town where you live? These two services allow local experts to offer unique tours to travelers and locals alike.

SHAREABLE FARMING – Become a WWOOF-er for fun but not profit. WWOOF, which stands for Willing Worker on Organic Farm is a great way to learn how to grow food while getting a roof over your head and meals covered while you travel.

Why Shareable Travel?

Travelers often stay entirely within tourist zones, and sometimes they don't even venture outside the restaurants, malls, and attractions mentioned in their guidebooks. To that we say, "Neighborhoods are where the action is." Neighborhoods are where people live (literally) and thus they capture the heart and soul of a place. When you travel using the sharing economy, you'll get a real taste for everyday life through the eyes and experiences of people who actually live there. And from then on you'll feel more like a traveler and less like a tourist.

From, say, late night outings in Milan with a Couchsurfing host to sailing on that 40' yacht listed for overnight trips through Airbnb, this chapter will shed light on how you can save money, meet new people, and have outrageously fun, unique experiences with congenial locals. Once you learn how to travel the interpersonal way, you'll never want to travel the old way again.

So keep an open mind about nixing those sterile and expensive hotel rooms. With a Shareable Travel life, there are no more boring nights of people-watching in the hotel bar or wishing you had a buddy along so you could get out there and do something.

Whether you're an executive attending a conference, a money-strapped entrepreneur, your basic budget traveler, a honeymooning couple, or just someone with a sense of adventure, you'll find something in this chapter to help you find accommodations, food, activities, and people to make your trip more affordable, memorable, and fun.

How to Travel in Style Using Airbnb

Airbnb.com

Type of Exchange	Sharing Components
Rent	Underutilized Resource
	Peer to Peer
	Save Money

As cities become larger and denser, prime real estate and the costs of doing business become increasingly more expensive. For example, hotel rooms in San Francisco go for a nightly average of $309; in New York it's $345; and in Hong Kong you'll pay $395. There are fewer and fewer travel options for those of us without deep pockets. But there is a way you can have that posh vacation of your dreams without shelling out thousands of dollars for accommodations.

Enter Airbnb.com, which allows you to book a couch, a bedroom, or an entire place at a price you can afford. Airbnb is a revolution of trust and a cultural shift to sharing what has been previously considered sacrosanct: your personal space. Airbnb gives consumers more and varied options for accommodations that are roomier, more comfortable, better located, more unique, and even downright decadent. The options (particularly in larger cities) are nearly endless. You can rent a spare bedroom in someone's house, or possibly a tree house in their backyard, or a luxury yacht, or perhaps that French castle you saw in a magazine. Some places come with well-equipped kitchens, full refrigerators, and jaw-dropping city views. And if you're sharing the space, you can end up making new friends with your host who often volunteers to be your tour guide. We'll discuss Airbnb from the "host" side in the "Shareable House" section, and focus here on using Airbnb as a guest for all of its awesome travel benefits.

Airbnb is more than just a simple value proposition - it connects people to people. Who you are (as both guest and host) matters as much as the rented space itself. Both parties get to "meet" online before doing business and get answers to questions like: Why should I trust you? What does social media indicate about you? How many Facebook friends do you have? Contacts on LinkedIn? Followers on Twitter? What do people who know you say about you? And most importantly, what do the people who have previously stayed with you have to say?

Guests and hosts are held accountable to their own reputation and as such people tend to be the best guest or host possible. When you stay in someone's home, you have the possibility of connecting on a more personal level. There's a natural tendency to want to help one another. Maybe you're looking to relocate and your host can help you find the right neighborhood. Or perhaps you're opening a satellite office for your business and want to stay with a local entrepreneur to help get plugged into the local business community. You can get so much more than just space when you use Airbnb.

Your space is limited, our resources are limited, and hotels are expensive. Your extra room is valuable. The time you spend traveling is precious. When you use Airbnb, you can exchange resources and all that accompanying value in meaningful ways. And when you do that, doors open up, often more than literally, so that trip, that adventure, that experience – even that bi-coastal romance – become possibilities.

So without further delay here's how you can best utilize Airbnb as a guest to get the most out of your travels.

How Airbnb Works

You login to airbnb.com and search by location and dates, much like you would to find a hotel room. Airbnb then returns results based on your query. You can browse through the locations and check out the photos, using their controls to filter by price and amenities. When you find a place you like, you can query the host about availability. Communications are made though the Airbnb messaging center to answer any questions, book the place, and pay for your stay. After that, you and your host can communicate about the particulars of your visit.

If you want to learn more, the FAQs (airbnb.com/help) should provide you with a good starting point before you jump into the guide.

Some Airbnb terminology you'll need to understand for this section:

Host – someone who rents a space to you

Guest – the person who requests and books a space (i.e., you!)

Introduction Request – a brief message telling a host who you are, why you want to stay with them, and your plans for the visit

Review – voluntary feedback provided by both host and guest after a stay has been completed – these reviews will display on both Airbnb profile pages

HOW TO TRAVEL USING AIRBNB

STEP 1: Create Your Airbnb Guest Profile

You can connect via Facebook or Google which will automatically pull information from your respective Facebook or Google profile and post it to your Airbnb profile, such as your picture, hobbies, and interests, all in one click. Or you can easily sign up using the form.

Add some information about your travel history, cultural interests, languages spoken, etc. to give hosts a better understanding of you. Remember that people rent to people, and your profile details often make the difference between a yes and a no. Be sure that your photo clearly shows your face.

STEP 2: Verify Your Account

Request references from your Facebook friends to give you greater "knowability": airbnb.com/users/references (you must be logged into airbnb.com to visit this page).

Connect to your social networks to verify that you're a swell person. Connect your account to Twitter, Facebook, LinkedIn, and any other groups you may belong to. The more verifications you show and the more completely you fill out your profile, the better you will appear to potential hosts.

Also add your phone number as still more verification that you are who you say you are. This is good for three reasons: your listing will rank higher, it adds an additional stamp of approval on your account, and it can enable you to get text messages about reservation requests. Note that you'll want to do most of your communication through the Airbnb website. This also creates a log and "paper trail" to better protect both you and your host.

And lastly, you can verify your profile with a photo of a government issued ID - this will definitively prove that you are who you say you are. To do this, you can either take a photo of your drivers license, government issued ID, or passport with you phone and upload it or choose to scan your ID with your webcam.

STEP 3: Find a Place to Stay

If your goal for this trip is to "live like a local," then look for those places where you'll be sharing the space with your host, much like you would on Couchsurfing. However, you might choose Airbnb over Couchsurfing to get nicer, more private accommodations versus just a couch. If you're booking a romantic getaway, a private apartment might be the way to go.

Head to (airbnb.com/s) to search by specifying the location to be visited, dates of your stay, and number of guests. You can filter the results by a number of criteria, the most important being the type of accommodation. Don't worry about price yet. Airbnb provides a map that shows the property locations within the destination city, and you can further refine your search by a specific neighborhood as well.

Review the host profiles on your "short list." Does the host seem particularly friendly or share your interests? Does their place have the amenities you need: wi-fi, parking, laundry, etc.? Does the host provide food?

STEP 4: Make an Introduction and a Request

Most host listings request that you send them an introductory note about the specifics of your trip and a few details about yourself. You'll want to write a meaningful, well-written request to let them know about you and to help you secure those in-demand places.

Note that all communication goes through the Airbnb messaging center. This prevents you from booking the place outside of their system and also protects your identity. You won't learn the last name or email address of your host until you have completed the booking and paid for the reservation.

To write a request, skip over the 'Request to Book' button and instead click on the smaller "Contact Host" button. This will help you open a dialogue with your host before having to enter your credit card details for a booking.

Tips for writing outstanding requests:

> ▶ Give the factual details about your trip

> ▶ Mention something in the host's listing or profile that caught your attention

> ▶ Share some interesting details about yourself like where you went to school, what you're passionate about, things you'd like to do in the host city, etc.

Here's a good example for an apartment rental:

Hey Chris!

I love your apartment! It looks roomy and the vibe seems relaxing and comfortable, which is exactly what I'm looking for during my next trip to San Francisco from June 12-19. I'll be attending the SES Conference (a nerdy marketing conference) and scouting locations for a new company headquarters. As you are also in marketing maybe you'd have some ideas for a 29-year-old female business-

woman in the cloud-based services area?

Are those dates available? I'll be the only one in the apartment and of course I'll treat it with TLC - I tend to be really tidy anyway. I'm also into Bikram yoga and can't wait to try out some ethnic restaurants in your Mission District neighborhood.

I look forward to hearing back,

Chelsea

Tip: Airbnb hosts get ranked based on their response time. Take a look at their response rate to gauge how active they've been recently. This also indicates how soon they may respond.

Tip: Check out the host's cancellation policies. If your plans are subject to change, look for something more "flexible."

Tip: Really read the host profiles. If you're allergic to cats make sure you review the "Pets" section. If you're on a working vacation make sure they have wi-fi and a printer.

Tip: Remember, unlike hotels, hosts are not obligated to accept you as a guest, so it's important to make a good impression.

STEP 5: Understand the Types of Hosts:

- ► Confirm Availability – these hosts request a short note with your arrival and departure dates/times before other communications transpire.

- ► Approve Guest – they request at least one initial round of communication about why you'd like to stay. When you finalize the request, you'll be asked for payment information and the host will have 24 hours to confirm.

- ► Instant Booking – Some hosts have enabled guests to instantly book their space, just like booking a hotel.

STEP 6: Book and Confirm

All guest payments and hosting fees are handled through the website. Airbnb accepts all major credit cards including Visa, Mastercard, American Express, and Discover. When you make a booking request, you'll have to input your credit card details. The host will then have 24 hours to accept or decline the request. Your card will not be charged until the booking is confirmed.

Tip: If you are confident about your trip dates and the place you want to stay, make the booking as soon as possible as hosts can get other requests or change their availability at any time.

Tip: Once a reservation is confirmed and paid for it's pretty difficult for the host to cancel. Airbnb automatically posts information about cancellations on the host's profile. However, as long as guests follow the host's cancellation policy, they will not be subject to any negative feedback.

STEP 7: Be an Unforgettable Guest

▶ Be Reliable – Communicate your travel plans by phone or email as soon as you get confirmed as a guest. Let the host know when you will arrive and make arrangements for checking-in at times that will work well for them. Keep your host informed about any flight changes or travel updates.

▶ Be Courteous – You're staying in someone's home, so make sure you don't make yourself too much "at home." Just because you're sharing a bathroom doesn't mean you can spread your toiletries all across the counter or toss your clothing all over the place. And think twice before making those pancakes at 2 a.m.

▶ Be Fun – This is especially important if you are staying

in close quarters on someone's couch or in their spare bedroom. Not everyone is social, but you can still show a sense of humor and be lighthearted when interacting with your host. Who doesn't like to laugh?

► Be Communicative – When you arrive (or before) make sure you ask enough questions to get the idea of your hosts day-to-day lifestyle and information about when they wake up, go to sleep, their house rules and/or expectations, any quirky things about their place, etc.

► Be Gracious – It's a big deal for someone to open their home to you. If the host goes out of their way to make you feel comfortable or cooks you a full-on breakfast, make sure you thank them. And if you can't thank them in person, a handwritten note goes a long way in our technology-driven world.

► Be Tidy – Leave things as you found them.

► If the place was spotless, leave it spotless.

► If you've been staying on someone's couch, make sure you at least fold the blankets. Like they say, little things mean a lot.

STEP 8: Write a Review

After your stay, make sure you write a thoughtful review of your host. This should prompt them to review you as well, which will make it easier for you to get hosted again in the future.

If you write an in-depth review, you will be more likely to get the same in return. Try to write a few sentences (a good estimate is 50-100 words) about what made your stay memorable. If there were any issues about your stay, we recommend addressing these with your host as soon as they arise, rather than includ-ing them in your review. Negative feedback will make it harder for the host to get guests. However, if anything made your stay uncomfortable or there were any gross misrepresentations, the review is a reasonable place to air your grievances and give other people a heads up. Note that you can also give the host private feedback (in your review) to enable them to become a better host.

"Airbnb Helped us Create our Business"

featuring Michael Radparvar of Holstee.com

In 2009, Michael and David Radparvar were jobless first-time entrepreneurs with limited funds, living in a two-bedroom apartment in New York City. They were starting a company to sell conscientiously-made, sustainable clothing online. But they wanted to do more than just sell cool products like 100% recycled tee shirts made out of plastic bags – they wanted to promote a lifestyle that empowers young people to own their lives, to explore, to travel, and to do what they love.

So when a friend told them about Airbnb, the Radparvar brothers immediately listed their second bedroom on the site and crammed into the other room. Within a few months, they were renting out the second bedroom for over $100 a night and were able to live virtually rent-free in their $2,400 per month apartment.

At times it wasn't easy to share and, as Michael recalls, Airbnb requires a "flexible mindset." Then he goes on to tell how Airbnb helped create the fabric of what was to become Holstee.com, "Our guests seemed to be in tune with the vibe of the brand we were creating, and in many ways even helped create it. One young woman designed an illustration that we used in our packaging, while others provided feedback and contributed to the overall look and feel of the website and the lifestyle of the brand."

Holstee.com became a known brand virtually overnight when they released the Holstee Manifesto, a modern-day "just do it" like reminder for leading a passionate, adventurous life. The manifesto includes phrases like "This is your life. Do what you love and do it often" and it spread to millions of people through Facebook shares and a viral YouTube video:

Holstee.com keeps seeing growth and is expanding their team. The brothers still use Airbnb.com to accommodate guests. "Airbnb has become a part of our lifestyle," Michael Radparvar says. Sounding excited about the future, he finished his story by adding, "The online economy is like the Wild West frontier. First, music; then publishing; and now hotels and brick-and-mortar businesses. All these industries are being shaken to their core by online services."

In the Shareable Home section, we'll teach you how to live rent-free as an Airbnb host.

How to Tour with the Locals
Vayable.com

Type of Exchange	Sharing Components
Buy	Underutilized Resource
	Peer to peer
	Save money

When most people travel they often do their own research online, use the concierge desk at their hotel, pick up tourist brochures in the lobby, or rely on strangers on the street to tell them about local events, happenings, and sights to see. This typically leaves much to be desired. Services like Vayable change all that by providing a platform for local experts to host insider tours, excursions, and events for both travelers and the general public.

For example, when you visit San Francisco you can book a $50 cruise around Alcatraz with a run-of-the-mill tour company or you can spend $30 to have a local history buff take you out on his very own sailboat and give you a two-hour rundown on the infamous Barbary Coast. Yep, you heard that right! There is now a growing peer-to-peer marketplace for unique and insider travel experiences! And these are not just limited to tourists – readers should check out the listings in their local areas for new and different activities in their own hometowns.

Here's a quick look at some of the San Francisco offerings:

- ► $37 for a three-hour street art tour
- ► $30 for a paella cooking lesson and feast on Ocean Beach
- ► $100 for a four-hour guided tour of the wine country

And for those "I've seen it all" tourists:

- ► $84 for a three-hour limo tour of all of SF's Medical Marijuana dispensaries

All of the Vayable "guides" are thoroughly screened through both a written application and in-person interview to ensure safety and to verify that their tour is actually adding something to the community. This process evidently works well since Vayable has close to a 100% positive review rating, which for a new company is way impressive.

STEP 1: Look Up Vayable.com

Start by heading straight to vayable.com.

STEP 2: Search Twice

Your initial search will simply include the location in which you'd like to have the experience. The most popular and exciting offerings will be displayed at the top.

If you don't see anything appealing in the initial results then try to narrow your search for a second go-round - filtering by category, reviews, popularity, and price.

STEP 3: Check Out the Guide or "Insider"

Vayable refers to their guides as "Insiders."

You'll notice that besides a profile for the tour/event there's also a profile for the host/guide. Make sure you look at both so there aren't any surprises.

A number of the profiles also have links to blogs or video snippets of past tours so you can really see what and who you're signing up for. Remember, you're not only buying, say, a four-hour tour of wine country, you're also buying four hours in the company of someone you hope knows a lot of interesting things about wine, wineries, vineyards, Napa County history, and perhaps some stories you won't find in the tour books.

STEP 4: Check the Pricing

Some of the events are priced for one person, while others are priced for groups. It can be a little deceptive when you try to book an "All Day Sailing Trip $80+" and then find out the cost is actually $800 because the price listed is per person for a minimum group of ten. The plus (+) sign indicates the average per person price for a group event. Note that if it's just the perfect wine country tour for four, then you and your partner can always buy up all four spots if you really have to go.

Note that if you want to go on a group event but don't have enough people, contact the host and see if there are any other partial groups that you could join up with.

You'll be asked for your credit card information when you request the tour, but you'll only be charged when the tour is confirmed. Vayable accepts Visa, Mastercard, and American Express. The cancellation policy depends on what the guide has chosen, so make sure you're both in agreement. Usually you're allowed to cancel without penalty at least 5 days in advance. Cancellations within 1-5 days are usually charged 50%, plus fees, and within 24 hours you will be charged in full. But check your local listings.

STEP 5: Ask the Guide What You'll Need

After you book the tour contact the guide and ask for information on what to bring, what to wear, and any other "nice to know" details. You don't want any last minute surprises!

For example, if you're booking an Elephant Trek in Thailand no website is going to tell you that in late summer or early fall you'll need to have insect repellent because the biting flies that follow the elephants will otherwise eat you alive. But a good guide will certainly give you that important factoid.

Or if you're booking, say, a summer walking tour of the old Battery Row in Charleston, South Carolina, the weather report will likely say "sunny" every day. But then you wouldn't be prepared for the 30-minute tropical downpour that happens almost every day around 4 p.m. unless you ask ahead of time.

You don't have to go over every single eventuality with the guide. A simple, "Hey, do I need any special clothing, shoes, equipment, sunscreen, etc.?" question should do the trick.

STEP 6: Write a Review

When you write a review on the website, it helps the guide to create better tours and attract more business. If you had a great time, why not share the tour on Facebook or Twitter, and maybe even brag a little to your friends?

Getting tours from local folks who are enthusiastic about their city, town, or neighborhood is going to be a more personal experience than booking something through a commercial tour agency. Your guide likely works in another industry altogether and simply wants to share his or her passions and insider know-how with you. Thus, your experience is bound to be completely different and more memorable than a canned tour. So try Vayable and tour like a local!

Other Options for Shareable Travel Experiences:

Sidetour.com
Zozi.com
Trip4real.com (limited to Spain)
Toursbylocals.com

How to Travel the World on a Backpacker Budget
Couchsurfing.com

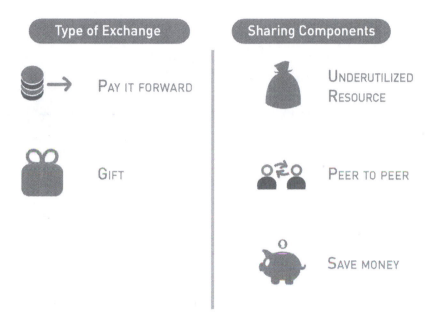

Poll a few people on the following three questions:
1. Do you enjoy traveling?
2. Do you wish you could travel more?
3. If so, why don't you?

Most of your respondents will answer the last question with some variant of: "It's too expensive." We're here to say that, yes, you really can travel more and for less money than you think.

The U.S. Bureau of Labor Statistics gives the following breakdown of annual travel expenses by your average American family:

As you can see, the average American family currently spends about 3% of their annual income on travel. It's a shame that number isn't higher but, hey, facts are facts. The more interesting breakdown is how we spend that 3%.

Let's assume you have a total yearly travel budget of $2,000, which would break out as:

Transportation-	44% -	$ 880
Food and Drink-	23% -	$ 460
Lodging -	23% -	$ 460
Entertainment -	10% -	$ 200
		$2,000 total

With that budget you could conceivably fly to Hawaii from the West Coast for a four-day weekend, stay in a chain hotel, and see a few tourist spots using conventional travel. The transportation expense is hard to mitigate since you'll be flying. So that leaves us with only the final three categories to adjust.

We're going to show you how to turn that four-day Hawaii trip into two different week-long Hawaii trips, or into a three-week adventure in Southeast Asia or Europe (or pretty much anywhere that catches your fancy) and all for the same budget by using Couchsurfing.org. to really enrich your life while you're at it.

So, that same $2,000 travel budget breakdown for your typical Couchsurfing member now looks like this:

Transportation-	80% -	$1,600
Food and Drink-	10% -	$ 200

Lodging -	0% -	$	0
Entertainment -	10% -	$	200

$2,000 total

Couchsurfing is an international hospitality exchange site with over 9 million members all across the globe which enables members to stay for free in other members' homes. Travelers can read member profiles and reviews in their destination cities and then contact potential hosts and begin a dialog to request a free stay. And often the host member may offer to act as your tour guide to show you around their city, help you avoid the tourist traps, and teach you something awesome about their culture. A seasoned Couchsurfer can often stretch that same $2,000 budget into a month's worth of travel and adventure.

The authors are all veteran Couchsurfers and want to show you how to use this service to make your travel dreams come true. They have created a full-length documentary film called "One Couch at a Time" that highlights Couchsurfing adventures all over the world. It was through collaborating on this documentary that they met and later became inspired write this book. You can watch the documentary at onecouchatatime.com to get a sense of what is possible when you share your life with a stranger.

First, we'll tackle the Couchsurfing guest, and later in Step 8 we'll add comments for being a Couchsurfing host.

HOW TO BE A COUCHSURFING GUEST

STEP 1: Join – It's Free!

Couchsurfing is free to join. The registration process is user-friendly and takes only a few minutes, even for non tech-savvy types. Register at couchsurfing.com.

You can either create an account using your existing Facebook profile or join with an email address.

Enter in account details and click "Create Account" to complete the process.

STEP 2: Create a Detailed Profile

After registration you need to create your profile. Remember – you'll be asking complete strangers to accept you into their home, so make sure your profile puts you in the best light. You can even think of it like online dating where you want people to be attracted to who you are, so posting a well-written, unique, and even humorous profile is important!

Once you join, you will see a status bar showing how complete your profile is - aim to get a score of 85% or better.

When you are writing your profile, follow the guidelines of "Travel, Trust, and Cultural Exchange" (see below) and you can't go wrong:

Travel

Everybody loves a well-traveled person with plenty of stories to share. If you've traveled in the past mention where you've been and include a funny story or two in your profile. You can also upload a few photos from your previous trips.

If you're not too well-traveled then just use this space to talk about your travel dreams, where you'd love to go, and what experiences you're hoping to have. Your prospective hosts want to see passion and excitement – give them some reasons that make them want to host you!

Trust

Trust is obviously one of the most important commodities in the sharing economy. To get the best of what Couchsurfing has to offer, you need to show that you're a legit and trustworthy person. There are four main ways you can increase your "trust factor" in the eyes of the community:

1) Profile

If your profile looks hastily slapped together with one photo and only a few lines of generic text, you will not be all that attractive to potential hosts.

2) Verification

Couchsurfing has a robust internal system that verifies your name, address, and location to prevent fake profiles. We highly recommend you go through all three levels of verification. The third level requires you to make a donation to Couchsurfing which also better serves to verify you. This will put a badge on your profile indicating that you have been fully verified by the service.

3) Member References

When you interact with other Couchsurfers they have the option to leave you either a positive, neutral, or negative reference. Think of it as eBay for people. If an Ebay seller has 500 positive and no negative reviews then you're likely to feel comfortable buying something from them. Couchsurfing is similar. When you stay with someone or go to a Couchsurfing event people will post references on your profile and you're expected to reciprocate. This is probably the most used mechanism for trust building on the website.

4) Vouching

This is the "holy grail" of trust in Couchsurfing. Well-established members of the community have the power to "vouch" for you. This is their public declaration that you are an upstanding member of the community and are totally trustworthy. This badge of honor will appear on your profile as well. Once you've been vouched for three times you can also start vouching for other members.

Couchsurfing takes vouching very seriously, so you shouldn't just arbitrarily vouch for everyone you meet. We personally recommend the "car" rule. If you trust someone enough to loan them your car, then they're probably trustworthy enough for a vouch.

Cultural Exchange

Do you speak three languages? Can you cook a tasty four-alarm chili? Do you work in robotics? Play some jazz piano? Did you travel the world as a military brat? You have a lot to share about who you are so make sure that gets put into your profile. On the surface Couchsurfing may only seem like a cheap way to travel, but underneath all that it's really about people. This is an awesome social experiment where people of vastly different backgrounds and cultures are able to share living space together for short periods of time. Remember, when you travel via Couchsurfing you are a representative of the people from your city, state, and country and it's expected that you represent them well. And if you can perform a card trick or two, so much the better. It's also good ambassador-ship to be inquisitive and interested in your host's culture (even if they're just in the next state over).

STEP 3: Join a Couchsurfing Group

Click on "Groups" tab to find out what's going on locally, This is a great way to meet fellow travelers as well as hosts in your area. Attending group gatherings will help you get references to start making a name for yourself.

STEP 4: Search for a Couch!

Depending on the city and the demand for couch locations, requests are often made far ahead of time. However, many hosts don't always plan their schedules, so even last minute requests can sometimes work.

To search for a couch, click on the search bar on the top of every page and type in the location of where you want to go, such as "New York, NY." When you're done filling in the location (make sure you choose "Find Hosts" on the left), simply click the magnifying glass icon and you'll see all the available couches. Once you do a location search, you can do a more advanced search using filters like: couch availability, verified profiles, number of references, gender, language, age, type of accomodation, etc.

Tip: Don't message a host who owns three cats if you're allergic. Some hosts want to spend a lot of time with their Couchsurfers; others are short on free time. The first step to having a good time is making sure your expectations match your host's, so you need to be clear about this. If you want someone to show you around town or help you plan a travel itinerary, then make sure you read all the host's information to see if there's a match.

STEP 5: Write a Legendary Request

When you locate the profile of someone you'd like to stay with, click on the button at the top of their profile, which will read something like "Stay with Her" (assuming the host is female). The message box at the bottom is where your legendary request goes.

Make it personal. No matter how many couch requests you send out, every single one should be personal and well thought out. Cut-and-paste requests are obvious and considered poor form.

Read every potential host's profile completely. Check out their interests, the languages they know, and the countries they've traveled. Keep your eyes peeled for any obscure song or movie references that you can mention to show you get their inside joke. When you refer to specific details in the host's profile, you're much more likely to get a positive response.

Here are a few other tips to help you write a great couch request:

> ▶ Talk Logistics – after you have them hooked with your wit and charm, it's time to discuss your schedule. Agree on your arrival and departure dates ahead of time to avoid any miscommunication. This is Couchsurfing, not "Couchliving", so be clear with the in and out points knowing that, like everything else in life, things may change.

> ▶ Keep It Short – most of the time, it's best to make a couch request that's just a few days in length and extend if things are going well. If you want to stay a week or longer, come up with things you could do for your host to help make life easier.

STEP 6: Surf Successfully

Aside from being a decent human being, here are a few tips that are good advice for every traveler, Couchsurfing or not:

> ▶ Communicate – give your host the detailed information about your arrival time and any contingencies. If your plans are still up in the air, that's fine. Keep them in the loop and work it out together.

> ▶ Contact Information – make sure to get all the phone

digits, the complete street address, and any neighborhood or district information. Remember you're not in Kansas anymore.

► Back-Up Plan – let's face it, stuff happens. If your plans fall through (which rarely happens with Couchsurfing) it's good to have previously established contact with a few other CS-ers· in the area who you might call or message in an emergency. It's also good to know the locations of local hostels before you arrive.

► Show Appreciation – most Couchsurfers like to do something nice when they're having a good experience. You can wash the dishes, fix their bicycle, cook a meal from your home country, or make an art project. Whatever you do, your host will appreciate the thought even more than the gesture!

No, there are no rules that say you have to host when you get home, but no one likes a mooch. At the very least buy your host dinner, or a bottle of wine, or bring them something cool from your homeland.

Tip: Never send a couch request unless you've thought about this question: Why do I want to stay with this host? If your answer is something along the lines of, "I arrive in Brussels tomorrow night and this person lives near the bus station" then you have some more thinking to do. Nobody likes to feel like a free last-minute hostel.

Tip: Avoid tourist behavior. This is the very reason and benefit to being a Couchsurfer. You have a wealth of local knowledge at your fingertips. Let your host take you to the local spots and get off that beaten path.

STEP 7: Post Couchsurfing References

References are the fuel that runs the engines of Couchsurfing. The exchange of references keeps the members honest and gives Couchsurfing its amazing track record for safety (5.6 million seamless Couchsurfing exchanges, and counting). References also serve as a virtual thank-you card (assuming you enjoyed yourself). You're limited to 1,000 characters so make them count! If you didn't enjoy yourself for some reason, you can choose to write a neutral or negative review, which will be viewable by all Couchsurfers.

STEP 8: Try Your Hand at Hosting

There is an amazing range of Couchsurfing hosts out there. Some host once a month or sporadically, whereas some power users, such as Emmanuel Lemor, have hosted an average of 318 surfers a year for the past six years. Some hosts provide king-sized beds in million dollar homes and cook for you and take you around to all the great sites. Some hosts offer an air mattress on the floor. Some will invite you to local events, some will offer trip advice, and some won't have any time to hang out at all. Some will even give you the keys to their front door.

None of these hosts are necessarily "better" – just different. You just need to determine your schedule and boundaries, clearly communicate that, and then attract compatible guests. Some helpful hints:

- ▶ Set Your House Guidelines on Your Profile – as a host, it's up to you how your surfers can and can't use your space. If you have a pet and need the door to be closed, make that known and everyone is happy. It's important to communicate all the details early on.

- ▶ Set a Clear Meeting Place and Time – also make sure you both have all of each other's contact information in case plans change.

- ▶ Be Informative – make sure that surfers understand how they should come and go from the house. Typically, you meet them at your home at the designated time and either give them keys, leave your door unlocked, or request that they return at certain times when you'll be home.

When your Couchsurfer arrives, show them where they'll be sleeping and all the "nice to know" information like how the shower works. Be clear about what they can and can't use: your computer, your phone, your kitchen, etc. If water or electricity is particularly expensive where you live, be sure to let them know.

► Discuss Expectations – let your Couchsurfers know how much time you'd like to spend with them, and when you'll be available. If you'd like to invite them along to an activity you have planned, tell them about it in advance. Also be clear about any schedule you'd like them to follow, whether that means a time to be out of the house in the morning or quiet hours during the night.

► Go the Extra Mile – think about helping the surfer meet their basic needs so you can focus on the real exchange. Do you have wi-fi, extra sheets, laundry available? If you have the time and the interest, taking your guests to interesting places in your city is usually appreciated. Some busy hosts make up their own local guidesheets to help Couchsurfers find fun spots on their own. Many hosts try to have dinner with their surfers at least once during their stay. Simply sharing your time is a nice gesture!

Tip: Express any concerns before leaving a negative reference. If you aren't happy with your Couchsurfers behavior, be sure to tell them why. In most cases, the problem is unintentional or a cultural difference. But if you don't speak up, your Couchsurfer might never know they've bothered you (or vice versa). But if lines are repeatedly crossed, it's your duty to warn the community.

In summary, Couchsurfing opens doors and makes you feel alive. Sometimes so much so that you begin to feel like human beings really are your tribe. There is so much to do, feel, learn, and be in the world – don't limit your travel experience to impersonal hotels and noisy hostels. Get out there – be bold – take a risk on a stranger and that stranger might turn out to be "a friend you just haven't met yet."

Other options while traveling include: tripping.com, hospitalityclub.org, bewelcome.org, and crashpadder.com. However, most of these alternative options don't offer as big of a community or what is known as the "Couchsurfing Spirit."

How to Travel for Free and Learn How to Farm Organically
WWOOF-ing

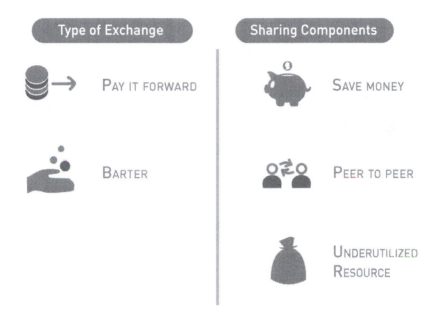

Type of Exchange	Sharing Components
Pay it forward	Save money
Barter	Peer to peer
	Underutilized Resource

What the Heck is WWOOF-ing?

WWOOF stands for Willing Workers On Organic Farms (or Worldwide Opportunities on Organic Farms) and is a loose network of national organizations in 99 countries that matches travelers with a farmstay in exchange for their labor. Travelers get to peek into what life on a farm is like and farmers get help from willing apprentices in exchange for food and housing. Typically, this is a barter arrangement where no money exchanges hands. Stays can be for a few days, weeks, or even years, if so desired. You can learn more at wwoof.org.

Many people become WWOOF-ers during a gap year. Students can get the opportunity to learn the local language and culture through agricultural work. But you can use WWOOF anytime at any age — on a short-term vacation or as a digital detox away from the hustle of a demanding job and the constant noise of a crowded city.

And it's good to note that WWOOF-ing is not only for people who want to garden or farm or learn organic, ecologically-based, and sustainable growing methods. There are also opportunities for those who are handy with tools, cooks, teachers, green builders, and just about anyone else with practical skills that can be used on a farm. An added bonus is that you'll likely be meeting fellow WWOOF-ers from other countries during your stay.

HOW TO BECOME A WOOF-ER

STEP 1: Become a Member of WWOOF

You'll have to pay $40 to access the online directory, or $50 to get a printed copy of the directory in addition to the online database: wwoofusa.org

STEP 2: Pick Three Locations

Farms near major tourist locations are notoriously full and hard to get into. If all the organic farmstays in Northern California are booked, try your luck somewhere else like Cancun, Mexico, which most people might dismiss as just a party town.

Tip: Be willing to work on smaller farms, as you'll likely learn more.

STEP 3: Decide Your Length of Stay

Even if you'd like to WWOOF for longer than a few weeks, it's best to suggest a shorter stay with the option to renew. That way you don't have an awkward conversation if the experience isn't meeting your expectations.

STEP 4: Send Out 3-4 Well-Written Requests

In contrast to Couchsurfing or Airbnb, which can often be booked at the last minute, WWOOF-ing stay requests are better sent weeks to months in advance. Include the specifics of who you are, why you want to come, how long you'd like to stay, what are you looking for in a farm, etc.

STEP 5: Communicate Your Needs Clearly

If you have allergies to cats or don't like animals, make sure you choose a farm that only grows fruits and/or vegetables. This way you won't be expected to tend to the llamas. In other words, get all the relevant details before you go.

Ask enough questions and set clear expectations with the host: How much work are you expected to do per day? How many hours per day? How many days per week? What type of work? Will you be given options for choosing tasks?

Make sure you cover:

- ► Food – are meals or food included?
- ► Housing – what will the accommodations be?
- ► Expenses – will you have to pay for anything out of pocket?
- ► Exclusions – is there anything that's not included?

STEP 6: Stay in Contact

Once you've agreed on an arrangement that works for both parties, stay in contact until you arrive. Make sure you have their mobile number, a working email address, and complete directions to the property. Remind them one week before you arrive that you're looking forward to WWOOF-ing on their farm.

STEP 7: Be a Willing Worker!

You're there to help, so be willing to pitch in where you're needed. Sure, you have an agreement but, just like life, being flexible is the key.

STEP 8: Enjoy the Spaces in Between

Enjoy the work, but keep an open mind about other opportunities. Many WWOOF-ers happily report learning new skills (e.g. how to make soap), finding travel buddies, picking up cooking tips, and meeting new friends. Be open to new experiences. You never know where your new career change may come from.

Tips and Notes:

► Bring work gloves, sun hat, sunscreen, sunglasses

► Also bring closed-toed shoes and clothes that can get mucked up

► Remember, you can stay for days, weeks, or months

► Anyone under the age of 18 must travel with a parent or guardian

► Note – there is no insurance or background checking provided - users should do their own due diligence, get travelers insurance, etc.

WWOOF-ing is an experience unlike any other. If you have an interest in gardening, farming, sustainability, green practices, or living off the grid, working on a farm might become one of the most memorable experiences of your life. Just think – you can enjoy organic meals, work a reasonable number of hours per week, have time to enjoy the beauty of nature – the sunsets, night skies, sunrises, cloud patterns, and the whole nine yards. Like the great philosopher Joni Mitchell sang in "Woodstock": Get back to the land and set your soul free.

Plus, you'll pick up new skills, meet new people, experience a completely different lifestyle, and learn about new cultures. And in these tough economic times, what's the "Number One Reason Why You Should WWOOF?" It doesn't cost anything (well, aside from that membership fee).

Other Resources:

helpx.net
volunteersbase.com
workaway.info

How to Swap Your Home for the Holiday of a Lifetime

LOVEHOMESWAP.COM

Type of Exchange	Sharing Components
Swap	Underutilized Resource
	Peer to peer
	Save money

WWOOF-ing and Couchsurfing might work well for the single traveler, student, or even a couple, but the sharing economy isn't just for the young and free-spirited. There are also amazing opportunities for families and those enjoying more extravagant lifestyles.

Since the 1950s international teachers and expats (i.e., expatriates — those who have left their native countries to live elsewhere) have been informally exchanging their homes. Now with the internet, home exchange networks have exploded, enabling people to more easily communicate and trade homes to enjoy cross-cultural vacations.

In a nutshell, the way it works is two like-minded families or individuals swap living spaces for a period of time, usually one to four weeks. These swaps can happen simultaneously or not, but typically you live in theirs while they're living in yours.

Retirees, families, and empty-nesters love the idea because if gives them the ability to live somewhere else in a home, condo, or apartment with similar amenities and to experience new places without paying the extra expense of hotels, restaurant meals, or, in many cases, transportation (the use of the family car is often included). Home exchanges are a great way to get introduced into the local community, since the swap partner will often provide insider information about the area and introduce the newcomers to neighbors and friends.

In contrast to a rental service like Airbnb, home swapping saves you money versus making you money. For example, Love Home Swap (lovehomeswap.com) is a members-only service that reports their average savings per swap is a whopping $3,487. And this enables 62% of their swappers to travel longer or take extra vacations.

Of course, not all homes are created equal. Someone with a popular apartment near the Arc de Triomphe isn't likely to want to swap for a home in, say, Baltimore unless by odd chance the Parisian will be teaching at Johns Hopkins for the summer. On the other hand, if you live in a popular destination like Manhattan, you'll have a much wider variety of offers. Like the old real-estate adage, it's often about Location, Location, Location.

This doesn't mean you shouldn't try for a home exchange if you live in a more remote area. Just be prepared to work a little harder. Also keep in mind that looking for homes in more "out of the way" locations may give you a unique opportunity to experience the "real" country away from the main tourist areas. For example, you may have a hard time getting that house swap in central Paris but if you arrange something in the French city of Lille, you'd only be a 45-minute train ride away from downtown Paris and you'd also have the opportunity to discover and explore some lovely countryside.

HOW TO SWAP YOUR HOME

STEP 1: Choose the Location and Dates

You need to decide where and when you want to go, although you can be a little flexible, such as a summer month in southern France. Having some leeway in your plans will help you find more arrangements. Note that most exchanges are done at the same time, but if you're, say, lucky enough to have more than one residence you may look for "non-simultaneous exchanges" as well.

STEP 2: List Your Home on the Major Sites

Some options for home swapping include:

- ► lovehomeswap.com (59,000 homes in 160 countries)
- ► homeexchange.com (55,000 listings in 150 countries, charges monthly membership fee)
- ► geenee.com (17,000 homes worldwide, charges for exchanges)

- ► homelink.org (one of the oldest home swapping sites with largest number of European homes, charges for membership)
- ► sabbaticalhomes.com (especially for teachers)

We like Love Home Swap because it integrates an easy-to-use website with a sexy design to give you that "Conde Nast" luxury experience.

STEP 3: Fill Out Your Personal and Home Profiles

- ► Profiles and Photos
- ► Fully fill out both your personal and home profiles. Describe who you are so that people can get a vibe for you. Be sure to include professional- quality photos of you and your home.
- ► Include the Details

Talk about the style and amenities of the house, the look and feel of the neighborhood, the proximity to local restaurants and entertainment, the number and size of beds, any safety features for children, the location of nearby parks, etc.

- ► Specify What's Included

If you have a pool or country club privileges, these could put you at the top of many swappers' lists. If use of your family car is included, make sure your insurance will cover the new driver.

STEP 4: Send Out Your Requests

Do your homework and conduct a thorough search in the area(s) you're interested in. Read the profiles completely and hand-craft each request – after all, you're asking to stay in someone's home. You'll want to be proactive and send out, oh, 10-20 swap requests at least a few months in advance. For popular locations you'll have a lot of competition, so be as personable and detailed as possible. Just like with Couchsurfing or Airbnb, your personality is important. Fight the urge to send out form emails. Think of your initial communication as the start of a relationship, so start off on the right (write?) foot.

STEP 5: Communicate, Communicate, Communicate

Ben Wislow, cofounder of Love Home Swap reports that "A home exchange is like dating. You have conversations, have Skype calls, phone calls and then you fill out an agreement form, which Love Home Swap provides. The property and location are quite important, but just as important, the people become friends and often exchange multiple times over the years."

FYI, Skype is a free software program that allows you to have video phone calls in real time. Once you narrow down the search to a few interested parties, in addition to sending emails make the time to Skype with them to discuss details, ask questions, and get to know the other folks a bit. If you feel like you need more information or reassurance, it's okay to ask for references.

STEP 6: Agree on the Swap

Once you find your ideal swap, it's time to formalize the agreement. With a service like Love Home Swap the forms are provided so all you have to do is fill out the details.

STEP 7: Fulfill the Agreement (i.e. Go on Vacation!)

Leave your house-swapping partner a complete list of details about your house, the neighborhood, your local contacts, nearby eateries, locations of grocery and drug stores, etc. Include all the how-to details for operating equipment like your washing machine, air-conditioner, spa, etc. Also make sure they'll know how to contact authorities, neighbors, or plumbers in case of an emergency.

Get your home professionally cleaned or take the time to do it yourself. Stock up on kitchen items, cleaning supplies, toilet paper, etc. Also, make space in your closets and drawers so that your swappers can unpack and feel right at home.

And then comes the fun part! When you get to the swappers' house, shoot them a message to let them know that you got in okay, ask any questions you may have about their place, and ask them to reply in kind. Take a deep breath, then start enjoying your vacation!

STEP 8: Be a Good Camper

You should be communicating with your fellow swapper throughout your stay. At the end of your trip, make sure you leave their place at the cleanliness level you found it, if not better. Vacuum the rugs, clean out the refrigerator, mop the floors, clean the bathrooms, tidy up the kitchen, wash the sheets, and restock supplies. Consider leaving a small gift like a bottle of wine or something from your hometown to show your appreciation.

STEP 9: Review Your Fellow Swapper

Who knows, you might do this again. Many swappers actually do end up becoming friends. In any case it's important to review them after all is said and done. This is best done on the swap website so that other people will know how awesome they are too. This should encourage your swapper to return the favor and review you and your home as well.

Home swapping is for the adventurous – people who want to vacation in a place that's more like home and less like a run-of-the-mill vacation rental. Unique charm counts too, as well as the thousands of dollars you could save. Anyone can be a potential swapper – even renters, as long as their lease doesn't prohibit such activity. If you own a condo, just check with your HOA to make sure a home swap is allowed. Many times, it is.

If you still aren't totally convinced that home swapping is for you, perhaps you should watch a romantic comedy called "The Holiday" where Cameron Diaz and Kate Winslet do an exchange and end up getting much more than just a new place to stay.

OTHER FUN WAYS TO SHARE TRAVEL

Where you stay and what you do along the way does matter, but so does how you get there. In the chapter on Shareable Transportation you'll learn more about how to get from A to B. But here are a few other options to enhance your travel experience.

Find Travel Mates

How do you go about finding new friends to travel with? It's often the case that you're the only one in your group who has the desire, time, and money to hop on a plane to that fabled exotic locale. If so, rest assured that there are plenty of other people who could meet you halfway around the world and journey together. To find potential fellow travelers, head over to travbuddy.com where you can also get insider information about your destinations from locals. This is a very useful free site where you can scan member profiles, find hotels, check forums, get travel ideas, write reviews, and obtain information on destinations from the "been there, done that" gang. As an alternative, you can also check out couchsurfing.com groups to find travel friends.

Meet People on Planes

Suppose you're the type of person who likes to meet people on the, uh, fly. Well, now you can literally meet them while you're flying. Planely.com makes it possible for you to be in contact with other planely.com members who are on your flight or will be at your departure or arrival airports. Knowing this information ahead of time makes it easier to serendipitously meet up, compare notes, share rides, and even become travel buddies.

Stay with Friends of Friends

Perhaps you're not comfortable hanging out with strangers, or sleeping on some somebody's couch, or meeting travelers in tourist bars. Maybe you don't even have a home to swap. Never fear – there is a hybrid option! Do a search on Facebook for friends who live in your city of interest and reach out to them directly. You can also put up a status update on Facebook and/or Twitter asking your friends and followers to introduce you to people who reside at your destination.

As you've learned, the ways and means of traveling are rapidly changing, making it easier to discover new locales, find innovative and less expensive ways to move about the planet, and provide the means to meet up with other travelers. To that we can only add, "All aboard!"

Shareable Education

"We've bought into the idea that education is about training and "success", defined monetarily, rather than learning to think critically and to challenge. We should not forget that the true purpose of education is to make minds, not careers."

-Chris Hedges
New York Times

EDUCATION

COST OF A 4 YEAR DEGREE

averages out to about $88,000 nationally and that number has been growing by about 5% per year on average

▶ ▶ ▶

+5%
PER YEAR

About half of recent college graduates are unable to find work. Of those who have found work half of them are working in a job that doesn't require a college degree.

$88,000+
4 YEAR DEGREE

Employers are less and less interested in your degree and growing more inter ested in what skills you actually possess.

List universities that offer FREE online education content:

FREE

- Harvard
- Stanford
- MIT
- Yale
- Princeton

+ more...

You can take a Ruby on Rails computer programming class for just $20 on Skillshare.
The average starting salary for a Junior Ruby on Rails programmer is around $120,000.
Beats spending almost $90,000 for a degree only to work as the assistant manager of your local Old Navy store.

Education COSTS

Many people today are having to decide if a college degree is worth the price tag. The cost of higher education has risen drastically over the past few decades, greatly outpacing inflation. For example, the cost of an average college semester in 1970 was $358 which, adjusted for inflation, would be $2,052 today. However, the current average semester cost nationwide is a whopping $6,696, or 326% above the inflation increase. And in states like California, these costs are still rising at dramatic rates.

Adding insult to injury, as state and federal education budgets shrink, many institutions are having to reduce class offerings, making it more difficult for students to enroll in the courses they need to graduate.

Total student debt in America has now surpassed total credit card debt, for the first time in history. And this raises yet another question about the 500-pound gorilla in the classroom: does it make economic sense to go into serious debt to get a degree, given today's dismal employment outlook for those entering the work force? A bachelors degree in, say, philosophy is nowhere near as useful or valuable as four years of on-the-job experience. Note that some professional fields (e.g., medicine, law, engineering, architecture, biotech, education, etc.) do require a college credential to start, but many others do not. In this increasingly specialized and highly technical world, an 18-year-old who spent a summer teaching herself the latest web programming language may be more in demand than a recent college grad with only a liberal arts degree.

And this is just in the U.S. Throughout the rest of the world there are billions of people who don't have access to education and, for millions of others who do, the cost of advanced education is just becoming too expensive.

The sharing economy gives students worldwide an alternate way to become educated, to learn, to collaborate, and to grow their skill sets using free courses that are available anywhere, anytime, through any computer, tablet, or smart phone.

The new paradigm of education is based on a more and more DIY (do-it-yourself) culture of learning. Here you make up your own curriculum and learn those subjects that interest you. In this "buffet learning" model you learn skills and topics a la carte without the extra filler. Anyone who had to take "Physics for Poets" to fulfill the mandatory science credit on their English Literature degree can relate.

New "open education" resources are being provided by many Ivy League and other accredited colleges and universities like M.I.T. and Stanford. These resources include course videos and practicums that can be used for teaching, learning, and research, all freely distributed on the internet.

Make no mistake – college students aren't the only ones with the desire and motivation to learn. There are lifelong learners, unemployed and underemployed workers, retirees, stay-at-home parents, people looking to change careers, and many others who could benefit from access to these open education resources.

To get you started in understanding how a Shareable Education can positively impact your life, let's define a few terms before we dive any deeper:

Open Education refers to education resources made available to anyone without an admissions process, and typically accessible anywhere through online courses and other distance learning formats.

MOOC is an acronym for Massive Open Online Courses, and these typically use open education resources such as textbooks, video, and other interactive media to present the material. These courses often provide a community or forum enabling students to communicate with each other, and generally do not charge fees or offer course credit. However, plans are in the works to charge fees, provide proctored exams, and offer credit or certificates. An additional benefit is that comments can be crowdsourced; that is, every student responding in the online forums can vote comments up or down, thus enabling instructors to tailor course material based on student feedback. San Jose State University is currently testing a couple of pilot programs which are achieving high success rates by providing 24/7 online mentors and even adding some in-class sessions.

Creative Commons / Copy Left (see Shareable Creativity) provide a legal framework whereby anyone can produce educational content or textbooks and distribute them freely.

Skill Sharing allows people who have specific skills or knowledge to share this information with others in classrooms, individually one-on-one, online, or any combination of these.

Anyone who is interested in expanding their knowledge or learning new skills for practical, professional, or creative reasons can benefit from a Shareable Education. We'll show you how to do everything from taking free Ivy League courses to teaching others what you know and getting paid for it.

How to Take Free Ivy League Courses Online

Type of Exchange	Sharing Components
Gift	Save Money

Thanks to the internet and forward-thinking administrators and professors, now anyone can take Ivy League (and other) courses from anywhere at anytime, regardless of the student's location, age, or life stage. Many prestigious colleges and universities have opened their courseware to students online, oftentimes free of charge. This movement has been referred to as open education or university 2.0.

Aided by the accessibility of the internet, widespread distribution of video, automated grading, and mobile technologies, online education is becoming a viable alternative to a traditional brick-and-mortar college program. These new education tools can also be utilized to leapfrog into new skill sets within the realms of engineering, design, science, and many other disciplines.

That said, note that an online course is even easier to ditch than one you're taking in a college classroom, so you're going to need a significant goal or reason for wanting this newfound knowledge. Do you want to move into a different profession? Learn a new skill set? Help grow your business? There is nothing wrong with learning just for the sake of knowledge, but having actionable goals and solid reasons for that knowledge will help you stay motivated.

STEP 1: Getting Started

Here are a few exploratory questions to ask yourself:

► **The What**
If you could learn something new, what would it be?

► **The Why**
Will this new skill be useful in your current profession? Do you want to pursue a new endeavor? Just want to learn?

► **The Where**
Where do you find all the information?

► **The How**
How will you make and manage the time in your busy life to do this work?

► **The Who**
Do you have a friend, peer, or family member who will work with you, help you study, and keep you accountable to deadlines?

STEP 2: Do Your Research

M.I.T. OpenCourseware (ocw.mit.edu)

All of the undergraduate and graduate programs taught by M.I.T. are accessible online, however students don't get access to professors or earn M.I.T. credits.

Open Yale Courses (oyc.yale.edu)

Yale also offers free access to introductory courses like astronomy, philosophy, chemistry, history, sociology, economics, religious studies, etc.

Stanford Engineering Everywhere (see.stanford.edu)

Ten courses from the Stanford School of Engineering are posted for free online.

Khan Academy (khanacademy.org)

Khan Academy is a university-independent online learning portal where all manner of subjects are taught. It is a great resource for children too. The TV show Sixty Minutes devoted a long segment to this amazing program.

Other University Courses (edx.org)

Check the website for other courses from Harvard, U. C. Berkeley, Rice, and other institutions.

iTunes-U (apple.com/support/itunes-u/using)

Even Apple is getting into the market. You can login to iTunes-U for free and access "the world's largest online catalog of free education content" with your Apple device. Lectures, classes, and even entire textbooks are available there.

STEP 3: Choose Your Course

Once you've determined what's out there, you can make a more informed decision on which class would be best for you. When you're first getting started with online education, it's advisable to start and finish one course before attempting multiple courses. That will give you more time to establish and instill your training disciplines and thus give you a better chance to succeed.

Here are just a few examples of Ivy League-type courses you could take:

- ► Harvard: Human Health and Global Environmental Change
- ► M.I.T.: Introduction to Computer Science and Programming
- ► Yale: Frontiers of Biomedical Engineering

STEP 4: Create a Support System

Recruit an Accountability Buddy

You can engage a friend, family member, fellow student, mentor, or coach to help guide and advise you during the course. It's even better if this person can also help you when you're stuck. The best option, though, is to find someone who also wants to take the course; that way you'll have someone in the trenches with you. You can work together on a regular basis, help mentor each other, and keep you both on track. If no one in your immediate social circle is interested, post the course to Facebook with an invitation to join you. Depending on the course, you may also be able to find and hook up with another student already enrolled.

Find or Create an Accountability Group

For many open education courses, you can find a study group or partners who are taking the same class at the same time. When you register for the course, there may be information on a class forum or other means to keep in touch with your fellow students. If so, take the initiative to contact others. If there is no way to contact other students, consider forming a general group on Meetup.com for DIY education students in your hometown.

Check in Regularly

Check in with your accountability buddy or group at least once per week. Tell them what you're working on and what you've accomplished. If possible, ask for feedback. Establish milestones for completing the course so you can gauge your progress.

STEP 5: Apply What You've Learned

If you take a course on how to build a more efficient website, use this information to imbed links into your blog, help fund your startup, or grow your business. At the very least, apply these new skills to projects you're working on now or map out ways to use this information in the near future.

You can also write about what you're learning to really get it to sink in. This may enable you to teach others or help you in future job opportunities. Consider blogging about your course to display the main points and help others understand the subject matter. This not only helps them, but improves your online reputation as well.

STEP 6: Celebrate!

You did it! Now go out and celebrate with your friends. Who knows, maybe you'll recruit someone to take that next class with you.

How to Take a Course on Any Subject

Udemy.com

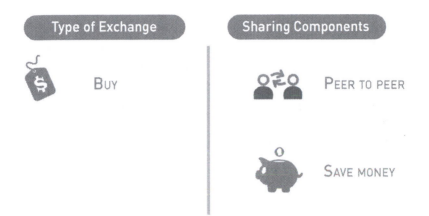

The beauty of Udemy is that anyone can teach and anyone can learn.

Udemy allows you to take online courses from leading experts and enthusiastic beginners alike. You can learn anything from "Ancient Greek Religion" to "Product Development at Facebook," taught by "Mr. Facebook" himself, Mark Zuckerberg. While both of these classes are free, many come with a modest price tag. You can take classes anytime and learn at your own pace, all by watching video lectures. Note that there is a wide variety of courses available for job and career development.

At this point you're not going to get an accredited degree using Udemy, but you can nevertheless learn new skills and spark new ideas by using the well-organized and easy to understand course materials. You'll learn more this way than you would by just reading occasional articles or watching short-form videos online.

HOW TO TAKE A COURSE ON UDEMY

STEP 1: Set Up an Account

You can sign up at Udemy.com with one click using Facebook, Google, or manually create a new account and add all the pertinent details. If you sign up using Facebook, feel free to skip the "Post to your friends' profiles on your behalf." You don't need that option to use Udemy.

STEP 2: Choose a Course

Once you sign up, you can search for courses using the search bar at the top of the home page.

You can also browse topics that you're interested in using the menu bar on the left hand side. All of the courses are categorized, so if you're into, say, Photography or Design, click on those from the drop-down list.

Click on the course title to view the course description, the cost, the details of each section to be covered, how many people are enrolled, the instructor bio, student reviews, etc. Use this information to decide whether this is the right fit for you. You can even watch a preview video clip.

STEP 3: Sign Up for a Course

Click on the "Take This Course" button to access the full course content. If the class is free, this is the final step for enrollment.

For courses that charge a fee, you can either pay with a credit card (Visa, Mastercard, American Express and Discover) or PayPal. Udemy has a fantastic refund policy – if you don't like the class, you can request a refund within 30 days for any reason.

STEP 4: Take the Course

After you login, click the button that says "Start the Course" and then click the green "Start the Lecture Series" button. Start with Lecture One and work your way through the video series. The videos will prompt you to look at any supplemental resources as necessary. Udemy recommends that the instructors make the courses approximately 60% video – so consider watching the video like attending a lecture class. Homework and other reading will be separate.

Most courses have a video series you can watch in succession along with text, audio, and other course resources. There will also be assignments and question boards for getting in touch with the instructor. If you have questions during the class, write them in the comments section of your course to the right of the teaching materials. This will prompt the teacher to respond and keep you in the game.

You can access all of your courses on the sign-in page every time you login.

Tip: Make sure you schedule lecture and study time in your calendar!

STEP 5: Apply What You've Learned

If your course was, say, How to Create a New Facebook Page, then take all your newfound knowledge and build one to beat the band!

How to Create a Course on Any Subject and Get Paid
Udemy.com

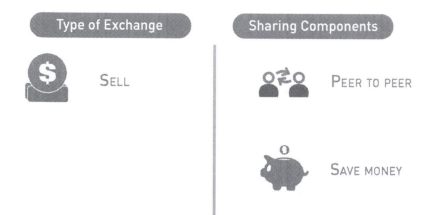

Type of Exchange	Sharing Components
$ SELL	PEER TO PEER
	SAVE MONEY

You can create a course on any subject, build your online reputation, share your knowledge, and make money all at once. With over 3 million members, Udemy has a widespread base of students. If you have a marketable craft or skill, you can make up to $200,000 a year explaining how you do what you do. While that's the exception rather than the rule, note that all of the top ten teachers earn over $50,000 a year, which is possible even by offering just one course. Note that Udemy takes 15% of the proceeds for administration and overhead if you refer a student and 50% if they are already a Udemy member or find the course through the Udemy website.

Regardless of how much money you make, teaching a course will help you learn your subject even better, build personal credibility in your industry, and enable you to connect with like-minded folks. Like they say, if you want to learn something, then teach it.

STEP 1: Start Here

Go to udemy.com/teach and review the extensive Help information at support.udemy.com

If you haven't signed up for Udemy yet, do so. Make sure you're logged in.

STEP 2: Pick Your Subject

Make a list of your skills, your interests, those topics you're passionate about, what you're good at, and the things for which people are always asking you for help. Consider which of those subjects might translate best into video format. Don't worry about being too selective. Just because you're the only one in your town who is interested in Cake Decorating, that doesn't mean there isn't an audience for it on Udemy. Also browse Udemy to see what other courses in your area are already available.

STEP 3: Name and Describe Your Course

To start the process, type in a title for your course and click the "Create" button. At that point, you will be prompted with a series of questions, which will help you plan out your course.

Picking a snappy course title is the most important thing you can do to market yourself. A good title is catchy, briefly explains what the course is about, and includes keywords which will cause your course to pop up on searches. An example of a good course title might be "DSLR Photography for Beginners."

The course description should include a brief discussion of the topics to be covered and what the student should learn from taking the course.

STEP 4: Create Your Instructor Profile

Explain who you are and why you're uniquely qualified to teach
the course. Include any relevant information about you or your
experience that will make students beat a path to your online
door.

STEP 5: Create and Upload Your Course

The best way to get up to speed is by taking the free course
"How to Create a Udemy Course" at (udemy.com/official-ude-
my-instructor-course)

Udemy recommends that your course should be 60% video
and 40% other materials such as text, infographics, photos,
examples, quizzes, etc.

The first thing to do is create an outline organized by sections
with lectures within each section. According to Udemy: "Lectures should be sequential, logical, and consistent under each
Section." You must have at least one section with at least five
lectures and at least one hour of video content to submit a
course.

Consider what other materials you'd like to provide as well.
Include exercises to reinforce learning, and possibly add things
like projects and assessments.

Upload and organize your content:

▶ Video: 1 GB size limit, use mp4, mov, or flv format at least
720p, for which most smartphones are now capable. Aim for
5-20 minutes in length for each video lecture.

▶ Other allowable file types: PowerPoint, PDF, MP3, Word
documents, articles, pictures, zip files, and YouTube, Vimeo,
SlideShare, Flickr, UStream feeds.

▶ Organize files into course "chapters" and "lectures" by drag
and drop.

STEP 6: Set a Price

You'll likely attract more students with a free course, but with
a paid course you'll earn 50% of all revenue collected (100%

less a 3% processing fee if you directly link someone to your course and they buy the course through your coupon code). The choice of whether to charge or not depends on your intent. If you just want to build an audience and/or disseminate your ideas, then make it a free course. However, if you want to make money then charge a "market rate". You can gauge how much to charge by browsing similar courses and then pricing yours accordingly.

STEP 7: Set Your Course to Go "Live"

Once you're satisfied the course is good to go, set the status to "Publish" using the green button at the top of the page.

If you are charging for the course, now would be a good time to apply to be a Premium Instructor and input your payment information at: udemy.com/user/edit-instructor-info

You should now promote your course using Facebook, Twitter, LinkedIn, and all your other social networks and professional groups. You can also offer custom coupon codes to lure in students and create a buzz about your new offering. The coupon codes give students set discounts on the course. Since the number of students enrolled is visible, you'll want to "prime the pump" with early attendees to generate interest and to encourage others to sign up.

"I Made $200-400 an Hour for Sharing My Knowledge"

featuring Kate Kendall

Kate Kendall knows a thing or two about community building. She successfully founded and ran thefetch.com for two years, a weekly curated guide that keeps tech, fashion, and design professionals in the know about what's happening in ten major cities.

Using her knowledge and experience, Kate also taught a Community Building class on Skillshare at her local coworking space where freelancers and entrepreneurs share office space (today, all Skillshare classes happen remotely online). Even with the 15% cut that Skillshare took, Kate made $200-400 for a few hours of her time, depending on how many people signed up. When she taught, she shared her know-how with those in her community, expanding her network and building her presence online all in one fell swoop.

You probably have your own skills that you could share in exchange for some dough. Skillshare is a great platform and an excellent place to post classes. However, it's not yet a great distribution network because most teachers bring in students from their own networks. So for now you'll have to market your class to your own audience on Facebook and Twitter or your blog (more on that later).

Skillshare can help you build an online reputation as an expert in your particular field(s) and can give you additional legitimacy in other areas you're working in or passionate about. Having consistently well-subscribed classes on Skillshare speaks loudly to your abilities. And this type of social validation can lead to well-paid consulting work, greater exposure for your business, and more clout in your field. Also, in contrast to just writing a blog or networking, you can connect with people specifically interested in your subject while you're getting paid!

You don't even need a business reason to use Skillshare. Perhaps you just want to have fun and teach people something new. Or you have excellent dating skills and want to teach people how to meet their soul mate. Why not? There are several popular classes on water coloring and there is even a course titled "Learn to Think Differently." The possibilities are truly limitless.

How to Share Your Skills Online and Get Paid

Skillshare.com

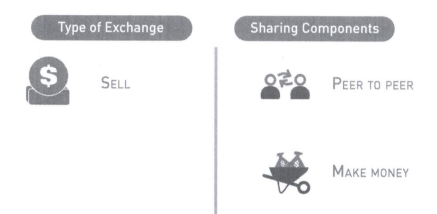

Type of Exchange	Sharing Components
$ SELL	PEER TO PEER
	MAKE MONEY

Skillshare was originally a marketplace for local residents to create course offerings online, which were actually held offline in neighborhood office spaces, libraries, and even homes (as told in Kate's story). Today, Skillshare is setup for online courses that take place in a virtual classroom setting with video content.

STEP 1: Choose Your Subject

▶ Teach What You Know

This might seem self-explanatory, but really think about what you're good at that other people would love to learn.

► Brainstorm a List of Your Skills and Talents

First start off with a list of all your hard skills and then move on to things people frequently ask for your help with. Enlist family, friends, colleagues, and coworkers to help you come up with a, well, classy class idea.

Try to list at least five solid ideas. Choose the one you're most passionate about or that will have the highest demand. Also, consider why you're teaching the class. If you're teaching to promote your business or personal brand, your choice will be obvious. Whereas if you just want to make new friends and have some fun, your options are more wide open.

► Do Your Research

Look around online and research your ideas. Is this class already being taught? Is there demand for it? If no one is teaching that subject, is it because no students are interested or because there is no qualified instructor?

STEP 2: Join Skillshare

It's easy to just use Facebook connect, but you can also create your Skillshare account and profile manually.

► Add a Good Headshot

If your Facebook photo isn't professionally suitable, then update it.

► Connect Your Social Media Accounts

When you connect to Facebook, Twitter, and LinkedIn, Skillshare can showcase how trustworthy and well-networked you are based on your other connections.

► Activate Your Paypal Account

Want to get paid? Well, add your PayPal account and you'll see payments each time a student signs up for your class. You can also sign up to receive credit card payments (Visa, Mastercard, American Express, and Discover) directly through the Skillshare website.

Note that courses are non-transferable and non-refundable. Students can request a refund directly from the instructor, but you are not obligated to do so.

STEP 3: Post Your Class

Once you're logged into skillshare.com, head over to: skillshare.com/teach

If you get stuck at any point, you can also learn more at: skillshare.com/teach/help

▶ Create a Catchy Title

Your title is a one-liner that gets people intrigued enough to read more and then sign up. Be descriptive, clever, and brief, like:

"Hey, Cool Shirt!": Designing Effective T-Shirt Graphics
Humor Writing: Become the Next David Sedaris
Facebook Marketing for Newbies

▶ Choose Course Category

From the dropdown menu, choose the most relevant category for your course. You can also choose related subjects by typing keywords in the "related subjects" box.

▶ Write a Course Description

No one likes to read long dense paragraphs. Try to write bullet points on:

- ▶ Why you're teaching the course
- ▶ How you're qualified to teach this subject
- ▶ Who the class is for
- ▶ What the class will specifically teach
- ▶ How students' personal and/or professional lives will be enriched

Note that you can also include a video of yourself to let people check out you and your teaching style beforehand.

▶ Add a Project Guide

One of the things that makes Skillshare unique is that each student is required to complete a project as part of the online class cirriculum. Write a step-by-step description for the project the student will create while taking your course.

▶ Upload Video Lessons

Click "Add Unit" and then upload a unit title and the video lesson associated. You can drag & drop the units to rearrange the ordering of the videos, if you need to. You can upload videos into the format of: mp4, mov, avi, or wmv with a maximum file size of 250MB.

Video Course Tips:

▶ Do Some Research

Consider taking a Skillshare class or two beforehand to see what others are doing and to get a sense about what works and what doesn't.

▶ Create Simple Visuals

When it comes to showing how something works, try to do so in the most simple terms so that students can easily process and understand what you're saying as you speak.

▶ Practice, Practice, Practice!

This is not only, as the old joke goes, the best way to get to Carnegie Hall, but will help you become more familiar and facile with your material. Start off in front of the mirror and then move on to your family and friends who can give you valuable feedback on your presentation, posture, eye contact, tone of voice, material content, slide readability, etc.

▶ Become a Public Speaker

Just as valuable as the course content itself, your delivery will make all the difference in how people listen and absorb the material. If you're nervous about standing up in front of people, consider joining your local Toastmasters (toastmasters.org) or taking a public speaking course at your community college or Adult Education program.

► <u>Publish Your Course</u>

Once you've completed all of the steps, including the uploading of your video course lectures, click on the "Publish" button to make your course publicly available.

Tip: If you're not ready to publish your course videos, make sure you click "Save a Draft" so that you can come back and finish it later.

STEP 4: Spread the Word

► <u>Announce the Class on Facebook, Twitter, and LinkedIn</u>

Post the class link and description to all your social networks and any local groups and clubs to which you belong. Encourage people to sign up and invite several hundred of their closest friends as well.

► <u>Email Family and Friends</u>

Ask your peeps to contact their networks.

STEP 5: Build Up Your Student Base

As more and more students join your course, you will build up your eligibility to apply for the Partner Program, which will enable you to get paid you for your expertise.

In order to qualify, you must teach 2 courses with a minimum of 300 enrollments between both courses. Skillshare earns revenue by charging students a monthly fee to take the courses, so once you become a partner, you will receive a percentage of that revenue based on the popularity and engagement of your course.

STEP 6: Apply for the Partner Program

To become a partner, go to skillshare.com/teach and click on the "Become a Partner" button. You will need to have a track record on Skillshare (see Step 5) or elsewhere to qualify to be a paid instructor.

Whether your goal is to share your skills, make money, build a reputation, create a following, or just have fun, Skillshare provides a great forum for those wanting to teach to meet those wanting to learn. Many people acquire valuable skills through their full-time jobs or passionate hobbies and can use Skillshare to teach others. It's a win/win for everyone!

HOW TO SHARE TIME AND SKILLS WITH YOUR NEIGHBORS
TIMEBANKING

What is Time Banking?

Time banking and time currency were originally created to assign value to people whose time and skills were typically undervalued, like the elderly, disabled, or uneducated. Today time banking is used by all types of people to build community, help others, and get things done.

Here's how it works: a person posts a request on the time bank website describing a task to be done, the time expected to complete the task, and the desired timeframe. Other relevant details are included, such as listing any special equipment, materials, or skills that are needed, etc. Other people view the list of requests and, if interested, then can make an offer to complete one. When a task is completed, that person earns the time bank hours specified (AKA "time dollars") and can then use those hours to get a task done for herself. Although the "unit of currency" for time banks is often called "time dollars", note that no money changes hands. One "time dollar" equals the credit earned for completing one hour of work and also equals the one hour debit paid by the requestor to have the task completed.

In time banking each person's time is counted equally regardless of skill or standard market value. The time exchanges don't have to be a direct one-to-one swap either. You can walk someone's dog and another person can help you learn French.

Each person will earn a time dollar for every hour of service performed. And you can even go into "debt" if you're just starting; you don't have to accumulate hours before you can spend them.

This concept is not new. Time banking originally flourished during the Great Depression enabling populations and municipalities to distribute food, clothing, and other needed services throughout the 1930s.

An icon of time banking, Edgar Cahn, a law professor and speech writer for Robert F. Kennedy, wrote an article in Futures magazine in 1989 titled "No More Throw Away People" where he outlined a society in which people could give back on an individual basis and have each contribution accounted for. Cahn's efforts helped time banking grow from isolated local networks into a nationwide movement made universally accessible by the internet.

In a recent interview Cahn said, "It starts with the premise that all human beings have something very special to contribute. There is a world of value other than price. So – I give an hour and I get an hour. The ability to find a match is made possible by this computer age."

According to Ricardo Simon of the Bay Area Community Exchange Time Bank, "Time banking makes the way we naturally share with one another more visible. After all, people helping one another is not a component of GDP."

Time banks are still mostly grassroots endeavors that most people are probably not yet familiar. Despite sounding like a hippie fringe movement, there are now more than 300 time banks across the U.S. Joining a time bank is a great way to feel a deeper sense of community, help people who live nearby, and create a support system for yourself when you, say, need a ride, need help moving furniture, or want some career advice. Really – the possibilities for asking for and receiving help on a time bank are limitless.

How to Participate in a Local Time Bank

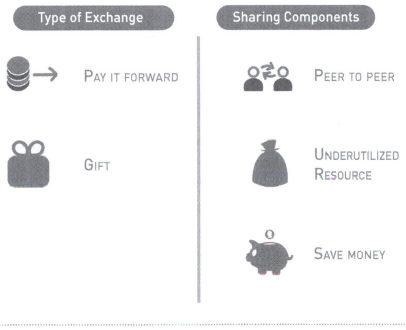

Type of Exchange

Pay it forward

Gift

Sharing Components

Peer to peer

Underutilized Resource

Save money

STEP 1: Locate Your Local Time Bank

Try a Google search looking for "time bank [your city, state]". Many time banks are independently run, such as the BACE.org in San Francisco, which has over 1,600 active members.

You can also check out community.timebanks.org where an umbrella organization has gathered information on time banks in the U.S. and abroad.

STEP 2: Create an Account

Once you locate the time bank of your choice, register for a member account which allows you to both request and offer services. Depending on the time bank, you may have to fill out an additional application or attend an orientation session to become an official member.

STEP 3: Find Ways to Earn Time Dollars

Think about what you're good at, as well as your work skills and any talents you've acquired through your hobbies or extra-curricular activities. Do you speak another language, know how to fix bikes, have a green thumb? Chances are someone needs you!

Examples of ways to earn time dollars:

- ► Teach yoga, guitar, dance, language
- ► Help with cooking, cleaning, childcare, elder assistance
- ► Give someone a lift to the grocery store or airport
- ► Coach on business, wellness, or sports training
- ► Repair car, clothing, computer, bike
- ► Listen to another person talk through a problem

STEP 4-A: Respond to a Request First

If you can, first offer to complete a time request before posting your own. This way, you'll understand how it all works. By initially giving back to the community you "pay it forward" which is in line with the spirit of time banking. Scan the list of available requests (usually grouped by type) for ones that you could do, or that are in your neighborhood, or that just sound enjoyable. Contact the person through the time bank with an offer to complete their task.

If your offer is accepted, coordinate with the requestor about the logistics and set a date and time for the work. After you complete the work, the requestor will credit your account for the agreed-upon number of time bank hours. You can now use those hours to "pay" someone to do a task for you.

STEP 4-B: (or) Post a Request

In most time banks, you don't have to earn time dollars before you spend them. Some people may need more help than others, so you're allowed to go into a deficit when you first start.

When you post a request, try to be as detailed as possible, such as "Need Help Moving a Half-Cord of Firewood from Daly City to San Francisco." Determine how much time the task will take. The time you post will be the amount of time dollars you will be debited and the amount of time dollars that will be credited to the responder.

List all relevant details such as those times when you're available, what materials or tools will be required, the desired timeframe to complete the request, and any other dependencies. The more details you provide up front, the less back and forth communication will be required.

STEP 5: Complete the Request

Once the task or service has been completed, credit the worker's account with the appropriate number of time dollars. Note that most time banks don't verify their members or their skills, so it's best to be flexible as to your expectations in getting your task done.

Other Time Bank Resources:

timerepublik.com
hourworld.org
community-exchange.org

WHAT'S NEXT IN SHAREABLE EDUCATION?

As jobs become more specialized, education is rapidly expanding into a do-it-yourself paradigm to meet the changing demands. The internet closes the gap between traditional education and the future of employment, both of which will become more flexible and less hierarchical. While universities aren't going away anytime soon, more classes will be taught online and students will be able to acquire their education in piecemeal fashion through alternative means. Once people realize they can be a teacher or a student for little or no money, the paradigm shifts from a top-down to a more democratized educational system for both the U.S. and the world. Just think, anyone will be able to learn from anywhere, regardless of national ties or economic class – all that's needed is a curious mind and an internet connection.

We recently met a few young students who have a progressive perspective on changes to the K-12 and the university systems.

Take 19-year-old Nikil Goyal, an author of the newly published book, "One Size Does Not Fit All", which explains how the K-12 system is failing. He says, "Every nine seconds, a student drops out of school. Why? For a majority, school was not relevant to them. The education system isn't broken – it's doing exactly what it was intended to do – create compliant cogs in machines. It's outdated. It's dangerous. And it's suppressing millions of children around the country." This book is a first-hand look at what many current policy makers, best-selling authors, and other renowned educators are saying. Many are proposing a thorough reevaluation of our current K-12 educational system to make it better and more effective.

And addressing the university system, 22-year-old Dale Stephens recently published "Hacking Your Education", a book on how students can literally hack their education with DIY resources. The book promises to "help you save tens of thousands of dollars on your education – ditch the lectures and learn more than your peers ever will."

These books, along with the growing societal questioning of our current education systems, will continue to give rise to open education. These online and ever-expanding resources mean that people can learn what they want, when they want, without bounds, restrictions, or economic barriers, whether they're a curious West African child, an American college student with limited funds, or your amazing grandmother in Peoria.

Shareable Creativity

"The creative individual is no longer viewed as an iconoclast. He—or she—is the new mainstream."

-Richard Florida
Author of The Rise of the Creative Class

Starving Artists Needn't Starve Any Longer

Shareable Creativity allows you to express yourself through art and design via the online resources that are available when you lead a Shareable Life. It's now easier than ever to make your dreams become reality, even if you're broke!

We'll start you off with some definitions:

CROWDSOURCING – To source (i.e., obtain or gather) information, design, resources, or feedback from large groups of people, usually through an online community.

CROWDFUNDING – A financial form of crowdsourcing which allows large numbers of donors to each contribute small amounts of money to fund projects using the internet.

MAKER – The self-assigned identity of an individual or group who envisions, designs, and builds physical goods in a do-it-yourself manner.

In this section, we'll show you how to get people on board to help your creative projects, allow others to access and repurpose your ideas (and vice versa), become a "maker" of cool things, use the crowd to design infographics for you, and create a viable business by marketing and selling your artistic creations online.

Networks like the Creative Commons provide a legal framework for people to access existing materials like written works, sound, video, and other mixed media and to use these materials to share, repurpose, improve, and redistribute them. They provide a structured, straightforward, and legal way to add to our collective body of information and to expand our individual capacity for learning and growing. For example, Wikipedia is a Creative Commons project.

Maker spaces, such as TechShop, provide the physical space and necessary tools to dream up, design, and build just about anything, from a programmable robot to a working prototype of your new electromagnetic-defragmentizer. Many of these spaces give you access to resources like laser cutters, woodworking equipment, sensors, high-tech sewing machines, design software like AutoCAD, and so much more. Whether you know what you'd like to create or just want to tinker around, TechShop offers classes to get you familiar with the equipment and possibly spark an idea to create cold fusion or build a better mousetrap.

Kickstarter, one of the larger crowdfunding sites, enables projects to receive funding from a broad support base. Typically, these projects would never have qualified for funding by traditional investors. Thus, worthwhile ideas live to see the light of day, and more collective dreams get transformed into reality. And the beauty of it all is that these projects don't necessarily need to generate a profit, save the world, or even build that new-and-improved high-tech mousetrap.

99Designs allows you to crowdsource graphic design work. You put your vision out to the online crowd and interested designers chime in. You get to review a wide range of ideas and designers get to flex their creative muscles and make some money, or at least add to their portfolios.

Websites like Etsy enable individuals who design and create art and crafts at home to connect with buyers online. This creates a worldwide marketplace and a public forum for expressing artistic creativity, whether it's in beading jewelry, making dresses, building custom furniture, or you-name-it.

We'll Show You How We Did It

This book is a product of both crowdfunding and crowd-sourcing. Since the authors are avid users of the sharing economy, we chose to "walk the Shareable walk" and use crowdsourcing and crowdfunding to make this book happen. Furthermore, we didn't even try to get a traditional publisher. We've written this book because we believe the future is shareable, and that we're passionate enough about it to not just tell you, but to show you how things can get done in the sharing economy.

How to Crowdfund Your Dreams
Kickstarter.com / Indiegogo.com

Type of Exchange

Sell

Sharing Components

Peer to peer

Did you know that, according to the Small Business Administration, 65% of all jobs in the U.S. are created by small businesses? In fact, 50% of our Gross Domestic Product is produced by small businesses – yet only 17% of these businesses ever receive financing! In the current economy, banks are turning down anyone who doesn't have at least a two-year track record. And even if a small business did manage to get conventional funding, the burden of paying back sky-high interest rates for credit could sink the ship. So, a lot of dreams have fallen by the wayside or have been left to only well-heeled entrepreneurs. That is, until crowdfunding.

Pioneering crowdfunding platforms like Kickstarter and Indiegogo are disrupting the traditional lending system by enabling companies to get a "crowd" of investors who each contribute small amounts of capital to fund a project or even a start up. A study from Crowdsourcing.org reports that in 2012 $2.7 billion was raised by more than a million individuals and businesses.

With crowdfunding, you bypass the middlemen and connect your fabulous ideas directly with willing donors and investors.

Besides the obvious monetary benefits, your crowdfunding campaign also allows you to:

► Test your market strategy

► Prove there is pre-sales interest

► Establish online presence and generate buzz

► Connect you with unforeseen partners

► Obtain a network of marketing evangelists (i.e., your backers)

► Raise more money than your target

With the savvy, tried-and-true tips below, you literally have nothing to lose. The only risks you take are the relatively small investments of time and energy it takes to create and launch your crowdfunding campaign, and perhaps the tiny dent to your public image if it doesn't reach its goal. Tim Ferris, author of "The 4-Hour Workweek," says, "I look at my network as my net worth." That has never been more true than in today's new gold rush of crowdfunding.

> "I look at my network as my net worth."
> - Tim Ferris
> Author of The 4-Hour Workweek

In fact, this very book you are reading was financed by a crowdfunding campaign. It would not have been possible without the 136 backers who believed in this project, wanted it to succeed, and put their money where their online mouths were.

HOW TO CROWDFUND YOUR PROJECT

STEP 1: Choose a Platform

There are hundreds of crowdfunding sites, many specifically aimed at tech, creative projects, charity, social entrepreneurship, sports, science-focused, photo journalism, non-profits, and the like. However, the two most-used platforms are:

Kickstarter (kickstarter.com)

Started in 2009, this so-called "all or nothing" platform has become the most popular, funding over 35,000 projects in all sorts of genres. Anyone with an Amazon account can pledge money knowing that if the project does not reach its pre-set goal by the stated deadline, all the money collected is given back to the donors.

This "all or nothing" strategy is a powerful motivator because it pushes the creators and their crowdfunders to cross that financial finish line. When we were creating the budget for this book, we really had to assess our networks, contacts, friends, colleagues, and potential audience and then choose our numbers carefully. Note that Kickstarter charges 5% of any successful campaign and Amazon Payments, the pledge processor, charges 3-5% for credit card fees. So we had to factor that extra 8-10% into our project budget as well.

Indiegogo (indiegogo.com)

Started in 2008, Indiegogo's built-in project categories include gaming, film, design, education, mobile, and technology. Unlike Kickstarter and other crowdfunding sites, you can

specify fixed or flexible funding for your project. For a successful fixed-funding campaign, Indiegogo charges 4% of the total
collected; if your campaign goal is not met, all money collected
is returned to the donors. For a successful flexible-funding
campaign, Indiegogo also charges 4%; if your goal is not met
you get to keep all the money collected, minus a 9% charge by
Indiegogo. Note that third-party payment processing fees of
about 3% are also charged by PayPal and credit card companies.

STEP 2: Determine Your Budget

Figure out the minimum amount of seed money you need to get
your project off the ground. Assess your social network and ask
yourself, "How much money do we realistically think we can
raise?" As unpredictable as hosting a dinner party can be, you
are often going to be surprised by unexpected people showing
up with bottles of fine wine – as well as those who had RSVP'd
immediately and are no-shows.

To determine the budget for this book, we first looked at all the
expenses we'd already incurred for meetings, research, events,
the promotion video, and our website. Then we added in the
costs of editing, printing, graphic design, shipping, and fulfilling
the Kickstarter rewards to our donors. It seemed reasonable
to pad the total by 25% to cover unforeseen expenses. Then we
discussed how much we thought we could raise versus how
much we actually needed. We settled on $7,000, and in the end
we raised $8,169, which after subtracting the Kickstarter fees,
left us with a deposit of $7,437 into our project bank account.

So, considerations that determine your project budget:

▶ Hard costs needed to make the project successful

▶ Fees for platform and payment processing

▶ Costs of fulfilling your donor rewards

▶ Unexpected costs and expenses

Tip: Break up large projects into multiple campaigns to better reach your funding goals. For example, Alexandra estimated the total budget for her Couchsurfing documentary at $27,700, but broke her fundraising efforts into pre-production, filming, and editing, and only initially campaigned for $7,700 to commence shooting the raw footage. So you might break your project into more manageable parts with well-defined deliverables. Rather than trying to raise enough money to start a business and make payroll for two years, start by asking for enough to build a prototype.

STEP 3: Create Compelling Rewards

A reward is a "gift" that you provide to your contributors. These are often staged, so that the rewards increase at specified price points, i.e., "the more you give, the more you get" kind of thing. Your rewards could be T-shirts, photos, downloads, stickers, the product itself (if you're creating tangible items like DVDs, CDs, books, widgets, etc.), behind the scenes access, or even time with your team.

One of the rewards we offered was a "Share-Over Make-Over" where we would spend the day with you, analyze your lifestyle, and give you a report of all the ways you could benefit and profit from various sharing economy possibilities according to your interests, schedule, and energy level.

Tip: Incentives, incentives, incentives. Unless your crowd will be your massive extended family, a rich uncle, or a well-heeled angel investor, you are going to need to appeal to the internet "man on the street". Some people are driven by altruism, but many more are nudged into action by incentives – so what would these folks need to receive in order to drop $25, $50, or even $500 into your collection bucket?

STEP 4: Create a Captivating Video

The video doesn't have to be perfect, but it represents how serious you are. According to Indiegogo's Slava Rubin, campaigns with videos raise 114% more money than those without. The video should have great visuals and a compelling pitch that fits into three minutes or less:

Express your idea simply, but get people excited from the get-go

- ▶ Use the right spokesperson to make the pitch
- ▶ Make your pitch in language and tone that fits your campaign
- ▶ Make your video both "show" and "tell"
- ▶ Explain how you and your team have what it takes
- ▶ Express confidence that your project will succeed
- ▶ Include "The Ask" – inspire your viewers with a "call to action" now to contribute to your campaign

STEP 5: Plan Your Media Strategy

Determine the length of your fundraising campaign – we recommend three weeks, or 30 days, tops. Counterintuitively, shorter Kickstarter campaigns are just as effective as longer ones. According to Kickstarter's own data, the majority of backers make pledges at the very beginning and at the very end. Remember, though, it takes a lot of constant communication to your network, backers, and possibly even the press throughout a successful campaign, so don't underestimate the time it will take to get results.

The better your plan from the beginning, the more efficient and effective your efforts will be:

Pre-Plan Communications

Have emails already written for the beginning, middle, and end of your campaign to keep your network informed. When your funding project kicks off, it can be overwhelming to individually answer everyone who responds, so have pre-typed emails and/ or a detailed FAQs section on your website to keep people up to date and, even more importantly, to save your sanity.

Contact Bloggers

Contact blog writers and have them ready to write for you – especially during the middle and ending periods of your campaign. Bloggers get pitched a lot, so find as many as you can through mutual friends on Facebook and write them cordial, personal letters asking for their help. You want your project to generate buzz and get legs to reach a broader audience and more potential backers. Make it easy for bloggers to help you by providing them with all the content, links, graphics, and pictures they need to get onboard.

80/20 Rule

Soma co-founder Mike Del Ponte raised more than $100,000 on Kickstarter for their eco-friendly water pitcher campaign. He used the 80/20 rule to ensure their success, which in this case meant that 20% of the stories about Soma yielded 80% of their contributions. Mike focused on contacting blogs and online news sources where the readership was substantial and the audience was relevant to their project.

Tap Your Network

Enlist a small army of friends and colleagues to start the campaign off with a social media bang. You'll be running a proverbial marathon, so it is your task to keep your team going strong from start to finish. Crowdfunding works by inspiring a crowd, and giving your friends a sense of ownership in the project will inspire them to work harder.

Tip: The time of day when you start the campaign will be the time your campaign ends. So, you may want to start, say, on a Friday at 5 p.m. when you know your people are awake and at their computers. Those final hours have been known to make all the difference, so plan accordingly.

Tip: Make sure you start your campaign when you have enough time to dedicate to it. Depending on the makeup and availability of your team, try to plan out X number of hours per person per week to dedicate to your crowdfunding effort.

STEP 6: Pitch Your Project Passionately

You've heard the old saying, "You don't get a second chance to make a good first impression." Well, it's even tougher here with 50 other projects simultaneously trying to make a first impression on the same crowdfunding site webpage. So how do you make your project stand out? Start by offering your campaign as an opportunity, not a handout. Be confident in your project and your campaign, create valuable rewards to entice contributors, and try to build in a "cool factor" to help generate buzz. Ideally, you want people asking you for the Kool-Aid.

Have your pitch explain:

- ▶ What your project is
- ▶ How your project will benefit society
- ▶ Who your team is – add backgrounds and credentials
- ▶ How much money is needed – show your budget
- ▶ When you need the money – build a sense of urgency, time is ticking
- ▶ How you'll ensure the project will accomplish its goals
- ▶ What rewards are given for each contribution level
- ▶ Why contributors will become "heroes" for "doing the right thing"

STEP 7: Leverage Your Social Networks

If you were not a social media butterfly before, you are going to have to find your wings now:

E-mail Effectively

Email is the #1 most effective way to crowdfund; then comes Facebook, Twitter, and blogging. Uber-creative types can also try guerrilla marketing techniques, like tear-off sheets on street kiosks, starting rumors, and hiring the Goodyear blimp. In any case, try to cover all the bases in your campaign's ballpark. Those who post updates every five days or less will raise four times more money than those who post every 20 days or more, according to Indiegogo's Slava Rubin. Heavy emailing efforts at the start and the end of the fundraising period will be your keys to success.

Tip: Seek relevant online media postings about the project and email progress updates to your network. Make sure the information is timely and important, so people don't feel spammed.

Tip: Always make the emails personal, especially to family or friends. Although the bulk of your email will be cut and pasted, start off with an extra sentence or two to say something personal.

Facebook Fantastically

- ▶ Get your Facebook network talking about your campaign
- ▶ Ask interesting questions that are easy to answer
- ▶ Post once a day (minimum) during your campaign
- ▶ Ask people to "Share" or "Like" your campaign

- ► Be personal and personable
- ► Release short video updates
- ► Don't forget a call to action!
- ► Relate current events to your campaign
- ► Use humor – share relevant jokes or Youtube videos
- ► Ask your audience to post questions, pictures, or stories about you

Tip: Did you reach any milestones or goals? Celebrate with your network by posting status updates!

Tip: Not many know this, but Facebook has a "Happiness Index" that shows a consistent spike in activity of 10% on Fridays. So take advantage of this by reaching out then! If you end your campaign on a Friday – ideally a pay day – people will be feeling grateful for the weekend and may be in a more giving mood.

Tweet Twittastically

This concise, micro-blogging, far-reaching network is perfect to remind folks you still need their pledges. Too many cooks may spoil the soup, but too many Tweets do not spoil the campaign. Au contraire, mon frere. Ask for re-tweets and thank your loyal re-tweeters. Use popular hashtags # time and again, and call your Twitter fan base to action!

Get Bloggers Bloggin'

Do your homework and find bloggers sympathetic to your cause. Contact neighborhood and city-wide hand-out publications. If you have a contact at a major newspaper, now is the time to call in those markers, if you have any. Search influential websites for topics that overlap your subject area. It's been said that there's no such thing as bad publicity, so get going.

Tip: However, don't send random emails to every media outlet in town. The goal is to appeal to bloggers, publishers, editors, media mavens, and that section of the general public who would have an interest in your work. Don't spam every big name in the blogosphere. One posting from the right blog is a thousand times more useful than irritating every other off-topic blogger.

STEP 8: Work Your Campaign

It's not exaggerating to say this should become your full-time job. If you want to reach your financial goal you are going to have to schedule the time, so roll up your sleeves and do what needs to be done. It's not sufficient to set up the platform, the budget, the rewards, the video (AKA your Academy Award Shortfilm contender), etc., and just wait for the money to roll in. You need to press the electronic flesh out there, put in the time to contact people, respond to inquiries, and then contact even more people. Pay attention to what is working, and especially to what is lacking. Your campaign is like a living organism. Ignore it at your peril.

Tip: Focus on driving as many people as possible to your campaign page. Many crowdfunding platforms use an algorithm that determines which projects get featured on their main page. This valuable visibility could well attract people outside your immediate networks to join the party.

Tip: You can use Youtube as a secret way to drive traffic. Go to a popular relevant video with tons of comments and put in a video response link or Facebook comment to your campaign video. A percentage of Youtubers will check it out. Youtube restricts you to one such video response, so choose your comment wisely.

Tip: Follow, up, follow up, follow up. Crowdfunding is a marathon, not a sprint.

STEP 9: Give Credit Where Credit Is Due

People love to be acknowledged, whether it's in the film credits, on your website, tagged in a Facebook post, mentioned in a blog, or even directly emailed (especially those people who contribute larger amounts). Let people know how much their help and support have meant to you. Of all your tasks enroute to crowdfunding success, this is one of the easiest to do and the easiest to forget.

Tip: Keep detailed notes on everyone involved. Kickstarter and Indiegogo provide you with a "Backer Report" which also has an Excel-compatible spreadsheet showing critical contributor information.

The Bottom Line: We are no longer limited by what opportunities are immediately in front of us – at any point any one of us can take on a previously unimaginable project, reimagine an entirely new business, or develop a prototype of an innovative invention. So, take that great idea off your "shoulda, woulda, coulda" pile and start putting up a crowdfunding profile. The world is your oyster – go find your pearl!

How to Use and Share Digital Media
Creative Commons

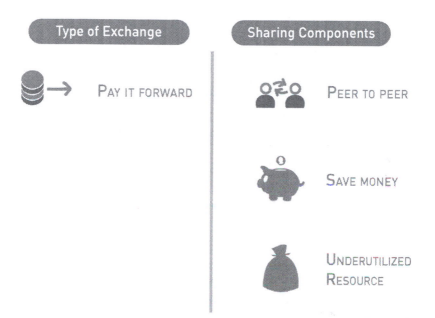

Calling all artists, creators, and researchers – and all musicians, educators, lawyers, scientists, writers, and others too! The non-profit Creative Commons (CC) organization provides a mechanism to allow people to legally share and distribute their work digitally through free, open licenses. These licenses are based on traditional copyright laws and allow creators to specify which rights are reserved for them and which are waived for other users.

Copyright laws state that everything that's published on the internet is inherently protected with all rights reserved for and by the original creator, and that to use copyrighted works you must get legal permission to do so. However, the Creative Commons licenses allow creators to specify usage and distribution of their works up-front by affixing "CC BY" attributions to them (see Step 1 below). This way, users are not required to explicitly ask for permission and know exactly how they can use, modify, and redistribute the materials.

The "CC BY" attributions make it easy to share music, images, video, textbooks, and other types of media. And since sharing media this way is so simple, anyone (including you!) can access repositories of Creative Commons works to help you create more interesting, rich, and robust projects which build on what's already available. This saves you from having to re-create the "wheel" every time and allows you to concentrate more on the "passenger compartment" of your project.

A stated goal of the Creative Commons organization is to "increase the amount of creativity (cultural, educational, and scientific content) available in 'the commons' – the body of work that is available to the public for free and legal sharing, use repurposing, and remixing."

HOW TO SHARE YOUR WORK WITH A CREATIVE COMMONS LICENSE

As a content creator it's important to know how you can: legally share your work, allow others to use and even expand upon your creations, add to the vast amount of shared media available online, and contribute to the benefit of society.

Given that you are the work's creator, CC provides six types of licenses that enable you to allow varying degrees of usage and redistribution by others. And as a user of CC-attributed works, you get legal access to them as defined by the terms and conditions of their particular CC license attributions.

STEP 1: Assign a License

Understanding your options will help you choose the best Creative Commons license for you. There is also a tool to help you decide, which can be found at: (creativecommons.org/choose). All CC licenses are specified with an attribution which further defines the rules for usage and distribution.

The six Creative Commons licenses:

1) "CC BY"

This is the most open license and this attribution lets others build upon your work and tweak it as long as they give you credit as the original creator or licensor. This license allows works to be used for both commercial and non-commercial purposes.

2) "CC BY-SA" (Share Alike)

This also lets others build upon your work and tweak it as long as they give you credit, and also allows works to be used for both commercial and non-commercial purposes. However, this license requires that any derivative works have the same license as the original, hence "Share Alike."

3) "CC BY-ND" (No Derivatives)

This allows commercial and non-commercial use of the original work as long as it goes unchanged and with credit to the original author or creator.

4) "CC BY-NC" (Non-Commercial)

This allows works to be used or modified, and then distributed with no restrictions. However, the derivative works can only be used for non-commercial purposes.

5) "CC BY-NC-SA" (Non-Commercial and Share Alike)

Similar to (4) above, except that the derivative works must have the same license as the original.

6) "CC BY-NC-ND" (Non-Commercial and No Derivatives)

This is the most restrictive license and does not allow a user to repurpose the content, only to share it with credit given to the original artist. These works can only be used for non-commercial purposes.

Note that there is one more specialized attribution ("CC BY-SA 3.0") which is similar to the "copyleft" and open source software licenses, and is the license used by Wikipedia.

STEP 2: Share Your Work

Use the Creative Commons communities (images, video, text, and audio) to share your work. Each of these have specific rules for attributing your works so they can be found and used by others: (wiki.creativecommons.org/Publish). Outside of these communities, Creative Commons licensed materials can be difficult to discover.

STEP 3: Post Your CC License

If you have a website you can post to your homepage or to the website footer the desired CC attribution icon, CC license information, and your personal information (for subsequent usage attributions).

Use the tool at creativecommons.org/choose to create the information and generate the HTML code.

Things to be aware of:

Must Be Copyrightable

Creative Commons licenses only apply to works that are copyrightable.

These generally include books, scripts, websites, lesson plans, blogs, other forms of writings, photographs, visual images, some data compilations, films, video games, other visual materials, musical compositions, sound recordings, other audio works, etc.

Must Have Rights

You must have the rights to the works. If you are the creator, you probably have those rights. However, if your creation was made as part of your job, generally your employer owns the rights.

Non-Revocable

Creative Commons licenses are non-revocable. You can cease your license at any time, but if people have used your content while under license, those works and rights cannot be revoked later.

No Registration

You don't have to register your works. Creative Commons is not a registry, but rather a set of definitions that sit on top of copy-right law and make sharing, modification, and redistribution of digital assets easier. Instead of registration, Creative Commons offers tools for attribution. Also included is the ability to insert HTML code into content, both human- and machine-readable, so that people and search engines can find specific types of content and licenses. (Note that these licenses are also described in three formats or "layers" – Legal Code, Human Readable, and Machine Readable).

For more information, visit: (wiki.creativecommons.org/FAQ).

HOW TO FIND AND USE CREATIVE COMMONS MATERIALS

Creating a video and need some background or transition video of a snowboarder in action? Writing a textbook on art history and want to find other lesson plans in existence? Or better yet, have a blog and want to use high-quality images without violating copyright law or having to pay for stock photos? There is a whole world of free, legally-shared photos, video, music, and text that you can use to make your own work sing. The Creative Commons has you covered!

STEP 1: Understand the CC Licenses

Review the six Creative Commons licenses as described previously or go to: creativecommons.org/licenses

STEP 2: Use CC Discovery Engines

To find search engines for Creative Commons works go to: search.creativecommons.org

FOR IMAGES:

► Google Images

Use the Google Advanced Search and choose the applicable Creative Commons license in the dropdown menu labeled "usage rights": (images.google.com/advanced_image_search)

► Flickr

You can search individual license types on Flickr by visiting the Creative Commons section and clicking into the "(See more)" link on this page: (http://www.flickr.com/creativecommons). And you can also do a Flickr site- wide advanced search and check the box to search only within Creative Commons licensed content: (flickr.com/search/advanced)

FOR SOUND:

Visit: (soundcloud.com/search/sounds) and choose from the Filter Results menu by clicking on "License to listen to" and selecting the Creative Commons license type you'd like to search for.

FOR VIDEO:

▶ Youtube

Do a normal search on (youtube.com) and then choose the dropdown Filters menu right above your video results and choose under the Features section "Creative Commons".

▶ Vimeo

To browse Creative Commons videos by license type, head here: (vimeo.com/creativecommons). To do a search for a specific license type and keyword, complete a search here: (vimeo. com/search), and click on the button for "Show Advanced Filters" on the right and then choose the license type you're interested in from the dropdown menu.

FOR TEXT:

▶ Freebase

(Freebase.com) has over 37 million topics and operates as an open source database – and all of the data is Creative Commons licensed as "CC BY".

▶ Wikimedia Commons

Wikimedia Commons searches millions of media files available through the Wikimedia Foundation projects including Wikipedia, WikiBooks, and many others at (commons.wikimedia.org). All content, text, and media found here is available for Creative Commons use under the "CC BY-SA" license.

▶ Google Webpages

To search for content that's licensed through Creative Commons on the web, use the Advanced Search on Google: (google.com/advanced_search), and choose from the usage rights dropdown the type of license you'd like to search for.

WHAT ABOUT PUBLIC DOMAIN?

The Public Domain is comprised of government compiled data, images, text, and video, as well as items added by citizens and intellectual property rights holders whose copyrights have expired. Public Domain essentially means that the works are not subject to copyright law, and as such are not part of Creative Commons. Public Domain works are generally publicly available and free to use.

To find works in the Public Domain:

(wiki.creativecommons.org/Public_domain)

STEP 3: Follow the Creative Commons License

This is especially important if you use materials with the Share Alike attribution "CC BY-SA", which requires that you share any altered content under the same shared license, in addition to providing attribution for the original creator of the works.

STEP 4: Acknowledge the Author

Be a great community member and go above and beyond to thank the original creator and let them know how their work helped you. Shoot them a personal email with a photo of your creation. You can follow them on Twitter and express your gratitude through social media as well.

A Case for the Creative Commons to Exist

Creative Commons is helping change education, books, and the cost of learning by making, in particular, major headway in the creation and distribution of textbooks. The average annual cost for college textbooks in the U.S. is more than $1,000 per student, which is often more than the cost of community college tuition, whereas the cost of printing a textbook can be as inexpensive as 75 cents. The Creative Commons has spearheaded an international movement toward creating open textbooks that can be used anywhere, updated frequently, and built upon as necessary.

U.S. News issued a report in January 2013 called "Governments Turn to Creative Commons Licenses to Reform Education Programs." Municipalities from Poland to South Africa are moving toward using open education resources made possible by CC licenses. It's just a matter of time before many textbooks in grade schools, high schools, and colleges are made collaboratively, translated into many languages, and shared internationally – thus helping to democratize education even further.

How to Turn an Idea into an Invention

TechShop

Type of Exchange	Sharing Components
 Rent	Peer to peer
	Underutilized Resource
	Save money

Have you ever wanted to:

▶ Rebuild a car engine?

▶ Program a robot?

▶ Sew a cocktail dress?

▶ Learn AutoCAD to create a machine-readable design?

▶ Weld an industrial art piece?

▶ Use a 3D printer to create totally cool widgets?

Hobbyists, artists, roboteers, entrepreneurs, students, arts and crafts enthusiasts! Now anyone who wants to make things can do so with TechShop or "maker space" programs. These facilities provide access to the tools, workspace, training, advice, and skills needed to make any vision a reality.

You can find TechShops all over the U.S. With access to over $1,000,000 worth of equipment under one roof, your creation is only limited by your imagination.

Much like a gym membership, makers join TechShop and not only benefit from the use of the equipment, but get inspiration and motivation just from being around other like-minded builders. TechShop offers a wide range of classes to help you learn new skills, and these classes can also be taken by non-members. There are even classes for kids.

To get access to the TechShop equipment, though, customers must first become members. There are a variety of individual, family, and corporate membership plans to choose from. For example, an individual recurring monthly membership starts at $125 per month. Before using a tool or process you're required to take its Safety and Basic Use class first.

Even if your area currently doesn't have a TechShop (www.techshop.ws), there are likely to be other maker spaces, hacker spaces, and tool lending libraries nearby that provide opportunities to learn and use new machinery and technologies.

And don't think that you're too young, too old, or not skilled enough to be a maker, builder, or a "do-it-yourself-er." The goal of a maker space is to help you discover, learn, and grow by realizing that you can create anything you can imagine. And most maker spaces offer beginner to advanced classes that employ hands-on learning techniques. Plus, the maker culture is very open, so you'll find that other members are more than willing to show you the ropes.

HOW TO BECOME A MAKER

If you're curious but want to know more about making before diving in, check out the Maker Faires (makerfaire.com) which are being held in the San Francisco Bay Area, New York City, Detroit, Kansas City, Las Vegas, and other cities around the world. These are part science show-and-tells, county fairs, and all-age gatherings of inventors, tech enthusiasts, artists, and other creative types to show what they've made and share what they have learned. You might also find maker TV shows popping up on your local PBS stations.

You can learn more about maker projects and news by reading Make Magazine online (makezine.com) or the Instructables blog (instructables.com). If you have kids, check out the DIY community and app (diy.org).

STEP 1: Locate a Maker Space

There are several ways to find maker spaces in your area, but your best bet is to first do a simple Google search for "maker space [your city or nearby urban area]". Many of these spaces are showing up in unexpected or remote areas outside of the urban centers where they first emerged. The maker movement is growing fast, so a Google search might reveal spaces that haven't made it on to other lists yet.

Also check out the maker directory to find specific locations in the U.S. (spaces.makerspace.com) There, you will find links to many of the maker spaces in the world. To use the maker map, click on the pins on the map in your location of interest. Additionally look for hacker spaces, which also provide project space and community (hackerspaces.org).

STEP 2: Take a Tour

Once you find a nearby space or two, call ahead and ask to schedule a tour. That way, you'll see what types of equipment they have, watch people actually working on projects, and learn about class offerngs. You can ask questions and get clarifications on how you might get started on a project of your own. Generally, the tours are free and will give you an inside peek at what being a maker is all about.

STEP 3: Take a Class

Many maker spaces will let you take classes without becoming a member. Some spaces even offer free classes or will allow you to win classes by writing up your TechShop project at instructables.com. Some classes may only be available to members.

STEP 4: Become a Member

Once you've taken the leap to visit the spaces near you, taken a class or two, and gotten acquainted with the maker world, you'll know if becoming a maker is for you. If so, go for it. Once you've become a member, you'll have unlimited access to the space, and hopefully you'll participate more often than you did with that gym membership last year. Signing up is your official entry into the maker community.

STEP 5: Meet Other Makers

One of the best things about maker spaces is the members! Once you're in and going regularly, taking classes, and getting familiarized with the equipment, you're likely to see some of the same faces. Be friendly and ask folks what they are up to (i.e., making).

STEP 6: Create a Project

Once you've gotten into the physical space, you may also find your mental space expanding about what you might be able to make. Immerse yourself in the creative process and add your new skills and knowledge to what you already know to design a new project. Starting small will build your confidence to take on bigger challenges.

If you want to get your chops up before starting on something of your own, consider helping someone else who's working on an interesting project. This is a great way to learn and expand your horizons!

Maker spaces bring creative people together – for example, an engineer may end up working alongside a machinist, which helps each of them grow and think differently. These spaces offer an intersection between art and science and imagination, and provide a hands-on platform for creating a more innovative, interesting, and rewarding world.

Maker spaces also offer an oasis for company team-building retreats where groups are able to bond while working on a wide range of projects. Opportunities to learn by doing are starting to show up in grade schools and high schools. Imagine ten–year-olds being taught to make things with their hands and then being asked, "So, what else would you like to create?" Help show them how, and then step back!

"It's a Shareable Life" Book Cover

A 99Designs Case Study

99Designs, which came out of a popular forum called Site-Point, gives upcoming and established graphic artists from all over the world the ability to compete for design projects. The way it works is this: a business submits a design brief to 99Designs outlining company information, goals for the design, any specific requirements, and possibly some suggestions on theme, imagery, colors, etc. Then 99Designs hosts a short-term contest to request submissions from designers to compete for the cash award specified by the business. The business typically chooses a few top entries to work with to fine-tune the designs, and then awards the prize to the one they feel best fulfills their requirements.

The advantage to the business is that they get to quickly choose from a number of mockups and ideas (for logo, website, pamphlet, etc.), and the advantages to the designers are that they compete for real-world projects, add designs to their portfolios, and possibly earn money by winning the contests. The winners are often offered additional follow-on work for the clients.

However, there is some controversy in the artistic community since there is a great deal of real work being done by many bidders, but there is (usually) only one winner. So the total amount of work completed far exceeds the cash dispersed (note that the winner gets 55% of the prize amount and the other 45% goes to 99Designs). All that said, no artist is forced to compete and these contests do provide great opportunities for new designers to get experience.

Instead of hiring some hotshot designer, our book team thought it would be a great idea to "walk the walk" by using the crowd and the new sharing economy to get the original cover art for our book. This enabled us to support the community of crowdsourcing artists, while saving major bucks in the process.

How to Crowdsource Graphic Design

Type of Exchange	Sharing Components

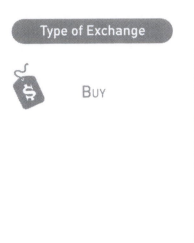

BUY

PEER TO PEER

UNDERUTILIZED RESOURCE

SAVE MONEY

STEP 1: Find a Crowdsourcing Platform

There are dozens of crowdsourcing sites to choose from, so we suggest viewing a wide range of public design contests to see what resonates with you and your business needs. We looked at sites like Crowdspring, Crowdsite, and a few others, and ended up choosing 99Designs.

STEP 2: Create a Clear Design Brief

You must understand your brand's personality, your business objectives, your target audience, how your design will be used, etc., to get the best results from your designers. Studying other contests and briefs is a perfect way to get inspiration and prepare you for your campaign.

We tried to be as specific as we could in our design brief in order to save time when reviewing the submissions.

STEP 3: Choose Your Contest Type

99Designs offers three price packages for book covers: Bronze, Silver, and Gold. These costs include the winning designer's prize, all fees and commissions, and their 100% money-back guarantee if you're not satisfied with any of the entries.

We chose the Bronze package, and hoped for the best. 99Designs requires that you pay for your package upfront.

Tip: The Silver and Gold packages will attract the higher-skilled designers and will generate more submissions.

Tip: If you offer a "guaranteed prize", this means you will absolutely award a winner, and this too will attract more designers and designs.

STEP 4: Launch the Contest

So once we completed our design brief, hit the "Pay & Launch" button, and filled out our payment information, our contest went "live." Our campaign would run for seven days, a time period set by 99Designs.

The contest begins with the Qualifying Round, the first of three stages. This stage lasts for four days and is open to all designers.

STEP 5: Comment on Every Submission

A total of 16 designers submitted their initial entries in the
Qualifying Round and we gave each of them specific feedback.
Although this seems like a daunting task, it's a common
courtesy to respond to everyone, given that they each spent
time creating a design. If their direction was good, we asked
designers to get back to us with our suggested revisions. Note
that comments to specific designers will only be seen by them.

Tip: Feedback is crucial to eliminate designs you're not interested in and to provide comments and ratings for those you
are considering. Although you want to be respectful of their
work, be hesitant to rate any submission at four stars or above,
because that may discourage other designers from entering
the contest.

Tip: Many designers wait until near the end to submit, so try
to create a sense of urgency to increase your submission
rate. All designers can see the submissions and your general
comments, so respond quickly and in detail to encourage more
submissions.

STEP 6: Enter the Selection Round

We then had four days to choose up to six designs. We chose to
work with four designers and at this point the contest became
"guaranteed" in that the prize money was definitely going to be
awarded.

Tip: Use your social media to put a call out to your friends and followers to vote on their favorites.

STEP 7: Enter the Final Round

We chose two designers to enter the Final Round. Then we had three days to work closely with them to revise and fine-tune their designs.

STEP 8: Select the Winner

Once the Final Round ended we had two weeks to select our winner, the design that best represented our vision and design brief. One design was especially sleek, the icons were unique and true to our brand, and the title font represented the 1950's feel we were looking for.

We closed the deal by selecting the winner, Audrey Jardin, and then we both signed the Design Transfer Agreement. The designer made the files available for our review. At that point we had five days to ask for any other changes, which are usually add-on charges.

Tip: Make sure you specify and receive the exact file formats you need for your design, so you don't have to tweak them yourself later.

Tip: When the handover process is complete it is good form to write a testimonial for the designer, which will appear on their 99Designs portfolio page.

How to Share Your Handmade Goods and Crafts and Get Paid

Etsy.com

Type of Exchange
- Buy
- Sell

Sharing Components
- Peer to peer
- Make money

Buy and Sell Handmade Goods, Vintage Items, and Crafts Supplies

Etsy.com is an online marketplace for buying and selling a wide variety of art, home furnishings, jewelry, clothing, housewares, collectibles, craft supplies, and more. With Etsy you buy directly from independent artists and can get such quality items as a one-off colorful bracelet handmade from Tibetan beads. And you'll never see your friends wearing one! Plus, you'll know who you're supporting with your purchase. Also note that many of the goods on Etsy are either sustainably-made or recycled from previously-owned items.

When you sell goods on Etsy, you'll connect with a community of other artists, enhance your creative passions, and make money by selling your goods to a community of like-minded customers. Heck, with over 30 million buyers and creative businesses, there are more than enough customers to go around – Etsy sellers grossed over $1 billion in 2013 alone.

Why shop at Etsy?

► Support independent artists and designers

► Purchase one-of-a-kind items

► Find creative inspiration for your own projects

► Request custom items (size, color, material)

► Less expensive than commercial businesses

HOW TO GET PAID TO SHARE YOUR ART

STEP 1: Decide What You Want to Sell

In order to sell on Etsy, your product must fit into one of these three categories: handmade items, vintage goods 20 years or older, or arts and crafts supplies.

Create and merchandise products that you love, and let that passion show. The more unique your products are, the better. Also the more products you post online, the better chance that product searches will result in showing your items.

STEP 2: Create an "Etsy Shop"

You will have to create a virtual store on etsy.com from which you'll be displaying your items and conducting your sales. With over 1 million active artists selling their goods on the site, your store and offerings need to stand out. Try to design for people like you, instead of creating something that might appeal to everyone.

For example, if you crochet, figure out how to add more "cute factor" to your baby slippers to make them more attractive. It's best to search the site for items similar to yours to get an idea of what's already on offer. Then do what you can to make your items unique for that particular audience.

First things first, you will need to sign up for an account, which you can do using your Facebook account or by manually creating a new account on etsy.com.

Once you're finished signing up, you'll be asked to name your store (you can change this later) and add product photos, titles, and descriptions (more on that in the next step). To open an Etsy shop, visit: etsy.com/sell

STEP 3: Post Your Products

Customers will be purchasing your items sight unseen, so give them a good sense of size, material, texture, color, details, special features, etc. Make sure you post at least one high-quality photo of the product, but it's best to have five or so photos of each item, taken in good light and from different angles. This will give people a clearer idea of what you're selling and make them more inclined to buy one, two, or a baker's dozen.

There is a guided process for adding an item which is fairly self-explanatory. You can choose product material, size, color, price, shipping information, etc.

Spend extra time writing your product titles, as this will either enable them to be found or ensure they'll get buried. So instead of naming your unique creation "Jennifer's Groovy Necklace", title it "Red Coral Necklace with Sterling Silver Accents". This better describes the item and should cause it to turn up in searches for specific jewelry items.

Tip: When you create your first item, make sure you click the button that says "Save as a Draft" before you continue to set up the billing information, otherwise you'll lose your work.

STEP 4: Choose Payment Methods

If you use direct checkout, you'll get 10-20% more sales, so we suggest you sign up for this. The cost for this service is $0.25 per transaction and 3% of the sale. This is in addition to the Etsy listing fee of $0.20 per item and 3.5% per transaction. To sign up for direct checkout, you'll need your checking account and routing number for direct deposits.

Other options for sales payments are PayPal, personal check, and money order.

STEP 5: Set Up Billing Information

Next you'll be asked for your credit card number to pay for Etsy listing fees, which are $0.20 cents per item to list for 4 months and a 3.5% transaction fee for sales. Etsy has no monthly or annual fees.

STEP 6: Verify Your Email Address

To complete the final step, you're asked to verify your email address so Etsy can contact you.

STEP 7: Review Your Shop

Put the finishing touches on everything in your shop. Check and update if necessary your profile picture, personal information, location, shop banner, all your items, prices, and details.

Learn more and get help at:
etsy.com/help

Review the Etsy Seller Handbook at:
etsy.com/blog/en/category/seller-handbook

STEP 8: Open Your Shop!

Click the "Open Shop" tab and then click on the green "Publish Listings and Open Shop" button to make your shop go live. At this point, you will be charged $0.20 to list each item for the first four months.

Tips for Marketing:

Use Coupon Codes

You can create custom coupon codes for up to 90% off or for free shipping. You can use these codes to promote your store to new customers on social media. Or you can create coupon codes that are automatically emailed to new customers after they make a purchase.

More Is Better

Stores that have 50-60 items for sale at any given time will do better than stores with two or three items. The more items you have posted, the more exposure you'll get because people will often come across one of your items when they are searching for something else. Also note that the Etsy search algorithm looks for items that have been listed most recently, so try to post two to three new things per week.

Use Social Media

Market your Etsy store on Facebook, Twitter, and pin your items on Pinterest. Also, consider creating a Facebook page for your Etsy shop and inviting your friends to "Like" it so that they can see your new products as you post them on your Facebook wall.

Be Creative

Use your signature to your advantage – have some marketing text automatically appended to the bottom of your emails, and include a link to your Etsy shop in all your active and relevant forums. You'll want to be working it on a daily basis.

Give to Get

Give away free stuff! That's right – find a well-established blog where handmade products are talked about and offer to give the blogger a few free products for a contest in exchange for a link and some publicity.

For more Etsy selling tips, visit: handmadeology.com

Etsy isn't a slingshot approach for hatching a new business overnight. However, building an Etsy shop can be a fun, profitable, and rewarding way to earn extra income, enhance your creativity, promote your art, and connect with like-minded people from all over the world.

Also see: artfire.com – an interactive handmade marketplace and crafts community.

THE FUTURE OF SHAREABLE CREATIVITY

Collaborative websites, do-it-yourself technology, and the increasing speed and bandwidth of the internet will make the previously unthinkable, well, now possible and even probable. From 3D printers in the home to collaborative workspaces to albums created by musicians who have never met, the future of creativity is exciting! Licensing and sharing media like text, music, and video through movements like the Creative Commons are just the beginning. And crowdsourcing as well as crowdfunding will expand far beyond Wikipedia and Kickstarter.

Crowdsourcing is already being used more and more by governments, businesses, and individuals to gather data, request solutions, obtain ideas, measure marketing and advertising campaigns, and generally get a wide range of feedback from the cloud. For example, a wildly successful 2012 Kickstarter campaign by Safecast resulted in the offering of small affordable Geiger counters to the public to measure and report background radiation. Visionary Jane McGonigal writes in "Reality Is Broken" that video games are starting to tap into the vast online problem-solving and collaborative network of gamers to help solve real-world problems in cancer research, oil shortages, global poverty, climate change, and the like. The SETI Institute (Search for Extra-Terrestrial Intelligence) has long asked for help from the public in unlocking the mysteries of outer space. So as to the future of cloudsourcing, the sky is, well, not the limit.

And crowdfunding is helping to democratize investments, conduct healthcare research, and bring myriad dreams into reality. Anyone can now participate in creating something worthwhile by contributing a small amount of money. A crowd of individuals can fund a startup, and cancer patients can solicit help to find their own cures. The internet and these new platforms are bringing entire new solutions within the realm of possibility.

The "maker" movement is picking up speed and providing a platform for all sorts of ideas to be shared among inventors, hobbyists, artists, technicians, and other interested parties. Places like TechShop are showing up in lesson plans at grade schools, allowing kids to learn how to design and create physical objects, while learning about engineering and science through practical experience.

In the future if you need a toothbrush, a wine glass, or a 3/8 inch bolt, you will be able to print one at home in real time! And the fun part is that the designs for these products will be open for you to use, share, build upon, change, and redistribute. To check out how to create 3D objects in plastic, ceramics, and metals, take a look at shapeways.com, which will give you a glimpse into this future aspect of Shareable Creativity.

Did someone say collaborative music? To learn how to create lyrics, songs, and music videos as a crowd, check out kompoz.com where talented artists from around the world can get together online to compose and render new music. The possibilities for creativity in the sharing economy could well be summed up in the lyrics of the old '80's hit by Timbuk3: "The future's so bright you gotta wear shades." We'll undoubtedly see much wider participation in the design, funding, creation, distribution, and support of projects and ideas that will form a new reality in which we can all be makers, artists, and entrepreneurs, at least to whatever extent we choose to be.

Shareable Transportation

"There are one billion cars currently on the planet, a number that's projected to grow to two billion cars within the next 20 years. We knew there must be a way to make our transportation system more efficient."

-Jessica Scorpio
Founder of GetAround Car Sharing

There are over 250,000,000 cars in the USA

CARS IN USA
>250 Million

AVERAGE $9,150 / YEAR

Owning a car costs you **$9,150 /year** on average.

The average SIDECAR / LYFT driver makes $20-30 per hour

The average Getaround user makes $300/month

The average Sidecar ride is 30% cheaper than taking a taxi

You can use Zimride to catch a ride from SF to LA for $30

2013:

TICKET

1.3 million parking tickets were written. That averages out to 3 tickets per every single registered car in the city or about $200 per car (it's like paying registration twice)

Here's the yearly breakdown:

- 48%: Depreciation
- 24%: Fuel
- 11%: Insurance
- 4%: Maintenance
- 4%: Tax

48%
24%
11%

Transportation COSTS

In urban areas public transportation has long supplemented and even replaced the need for cars. But now, given the sharing economy, what other options are out there? Turns out, there are quite a few.

Today the new wave of possibilities includes sharing rides, cars, journeys, bikes, and even parking spaces. This section will offer a glimpse into the future of Shareable Transportation and show you how you too can save money through ride sharing, make money by giving rides, make even more money by renting out your car, and even put that extra space in your driveway to good use. And if you live in a city, we'll show you how you can ditch your car altogether and best utilize these new cost-saving alternatives to getting around.

Most cars sit idle ten or more hours a day and most car owners drive solo, so right from the get-go there is a lot of capacity that is being wasted. New peer-to-peer transportation services make it possible to make money by renting out your car and/or giving rides to people – legally – and with complete liability and insurance coverage. Why make a long drive solo when you can invite other simpatico fellow-travelers to pass the time and pay for your journey?

Then there's the ultimate bane of city living, tickets! In 2013 1.3 million parking tickets were written in the U.S. That averages out to three tickets per registered urban vehicle, or about $200, which is like paying your car registration twice over. Fear not, Shareable Transportation has your back.

So, come on along for the ride...

SHAREABLE CARS

Cars are for most people their second largest expense, right after housing. And adding insult to injury, the average car spends 92% of its life parked.

With over 80% of the U.S. population now living in urban areas, car sharing makes increasing economic sense. People who utilize car sharing options are estimated to drive about 50% less, and thus are able to realize substantial cost savings. True, many people don't drive at all, relying on public transit, biking, carpools, and walking. But for those city dwellers who need cars, there are many exciting new options.

So what do we mean by car sharing? Today's options include:

- ▶ Renting a car in your neighborhood when you need a vehicle
- ▶ Renting your car to neighbors, coworkers, friends, and the general public
- ▶ Getting and giving short rides with private vehicles
- ▶ Sharing expenses on longer journeys with fellow travelers

One of the forerunners in that first bullet point above is a company called Zipcar, which incidentally announced in early 2013 it was being purchased by Avis for about $500M. Zipcar and other similar operations provide fleets of company-owned vehicles strategically parked in dense urban areas to make it easy for people to rent them for short-term use. To utilize these vehicles, users pay an annual membership fee and an hourly rate which includes mileage, gas, and insurance. Note that the car must be returned to the original location and that the pricing structure does not allow overnight or one-way use.

A more general model is the second bullet point: peer-to-peer car sharing in which people rent their privately-owned cars to other people. In this model, an individual can pay for a vehicle by the hour, day, week, or more.

Getaround.com, one of the leaders in peer-to-peer car sharing, was founded in 2010 with the intent to get a billion cars off the road by 2014. The good news is that by 2013, their fleet exceeded the total number of cars on Zipcar. By using existing assets that would otherwise remain parked and unused, Getaround helps keep down the number of new vehicles needed in metropolitan areas.

HOW TO MAKE $300 A MONTH BY RENTING OUT YOUR CAR

GETAROUND.COM

Type of Exchange

RENT

Sharing Components

UNDERUTILIZED RESOURCE

MAKE MONEY

Car sharing companies like Getaround and Relayrides, and others are changing the way people rent cars by offering peer-to-peer options. As discussed previously, in the sharing economy "peer-to-peer" essentially means person-to-person, as opposed to the traditional person-to-business model where consumers do business with established companies. A big difference between peer-to-peer car sharing and car renting from a brick-and-mortar company like Hertz is that about 75% of the customers are local, which often leads to repeat business. These peer-to-peer services allow owners to rent their cars to whoever they choose – friends, coworkers, neighbors, and social media friends, as well as to the general public.

Why Would Someone Rent My Car Vs. a Rental Car?

You might think hiring a car through a rental company like Hertz or Enterprise is the easiest way to go, but peer-to-peer car sharing actually has more advantages. First, consider convenience. Many cities have urban density issues, and often the rental companies are only located at airports or in the congested downtown areas, so your chances of finding a peer-to-peer rental close to your home or work are much better. Plus, you won't have to stand in line under fluorescent lights, filling out form after form. Renters can sign up online, enter their payment information upfront, and start driving your car almost immediately. In many cases, renters can pick up your car on the street and automatically unlock it with a smartphone. Also consider that car sharing gives renters more options – from the brand new, cutting-edge Tesla Model S to a van to move your Aunt Lilly's couch across town.

Enter Getaround

For the sake of clarity, the peer-to-peer car sharing service called Getaround will be used here as the example.

Getaround is a free membership service that allows people to rent private cars for periods of time by the hour, day, week, or month. Getaround also provides owner and renter vetting, full liability and damage insurance, and 24-hour roadside assistance. Both owners and renters are vetted and verified beforehand via DMV records, financial history, social media, and transaction reviews. Owners and renters are encouraged to rate each other after every transaction to better build their online "reputations" and trustworthiness rankings, both of which factor into their next transactions.

Cars may be posted up for rent during times when they'd normally just be parked in the driveway, or out on the street, or in a garage at work. Many urban car owners don't use their cars at all during prime daytime hours because they work from home or take public transportation to their jobs.

Is renting your car worth it? Well, the average car owner on Getaround takes home $200-300 every month, greatly defraying the costs of ownership. And car sharing gives renters more options to find transportation closer to them, with greater convenience, and at cheaper costs.

How Car Sharing Works

All well and good, you say, but what about those big questions: How is the insurance handled? What if I need the car and the renter is late bringing it back? Who pays parking or traffic tickets? What if I notice a scrape on the car? Who fills up the tank? What if the renter gets in an accident or injures someone? Who is responsible? And so on.

First, insurance. Getaround provides insurance coverage to both owner and renter to protect them in case of an accident, vandalism, theft, natural disaster, etc. That policy, separate from the owner's insurance, is set up by Getaround for the entire rental period and provides full comprehensive, collision, property, and medical coverage. And there's a big bonus – 24-hour roadside assistance is also included.

Next, income. The vehicle owner receives about 60% of the rental fee and Getaround currently gets about 40% to cover the costs of insurance, roadside assistance, and administration. For example, if a vehicle rents for $45 per day, the vehicle owner gets $27 and Getaround receives the remaining $18. The renter pays a $1 transaction fee to Getaround each time.

Getaround has a very comprehensive FAQs section, clickable on the company's main web page which should answer most of your questions.

HOW TO RENT OUT YOUR CAR ON GETAROUND

STEP 1: Gather Information

Provide information about you and your car:

- ▶ Insurance provider and policy number
- ▶ Pictures of front, back, and both sides of your vehicle (you can take photos on your smartphone and email them to yourself
- ▶ Vehicle Information Number (VIN) – found on your registration document
- ▶ Drivers license number
- ▶ A schedule of when you do and don't use your car (to fill in a calendar)

STEP 2: Sign Up

Fill out your membership profile at getaround.com

STEP 3: Set Your Rental Rates

Choose how much you want to charge per hour, day, and week. You can do this using the sliders. You'll want to be competitive with other cars in your area, so check around on the site for similar type vehicles in your neighborhood. Remember to factor in the 40% of the transaction fees that goes to Getaround.

STEP 4: Set Up Your Calendar

Indicate when your car is most often available. You'll always have the option to accept or deny rental requests.

STEP 5: Describe Your Car

Give all pertinent information about your vehicle. Make sure that you list any quirks regarding your car in the description area. If your driver side door doesn't lock or the car makes a squeaking sound at stoplights, you'd better mention that up front.

Car Sharing Tips:

Clean Your Car

Probably twice a month is best. Vacuuming and inside cleaning can be done as well to enhance the rental experience and perhaps allow you to charge a little more.

Sign up for SMS

This means Short Message System (i.e., text message) alerts to be able to respond to requests immediately. The faster you respond, the higher your listing will rank, then the more requests you'll get, and the more money you'll make.

Make It Easy

You want renters to be able to pick up your car with minimum hassle. For example, if your car is usually parked in a garage, be sure to inform the facility operators that other people will occasionally come by to use the car.

Get a Kit

Have the Getaround car kit installed to simplify the rental process! If you plan on renting your car regularly, you can apply for a car kit which allows renters to open your car remotely with a smartphone and get the keys from inside. If your car has Onstar it can possibly also be opened by renters.

Other Opening Options

If you can't get the Getaround car kit, consider placing a real estate lock box with a magnet underneath your car. When you rent the car, you can tell the driver the combination. If you do this, uh, you'll want to change the combo regularly.

Write Reviews

Always write a review of the renter after your car is returned. This will prompt them to review you as well, which will encourage future renters to choose your wheels over others in the neighborhood.

Contact Getaround

If there are issues, contact Getaround immediately. For example, if a driver doesn't fill up your gas tank to the proper level or causes any damage, immediately notify Getaround and they will rectify the issue. This is part of their administrative coverage.

Once you book your first rental, you'll be hooked! Handing over the keys to one of your most expensive assets can be both liberating and scary – just rest assured that you're covered in case of any accident, tickets, unpaid bridge tolls, or nuclear disaster. And if anything goes wrong, Getaround's insurance completely covers the rental period so your insurance will not be involved.

Car sharing is a win-win exchange whether you are the driver or the renter. The car owner pockets some extra cash and the renter saves money by paying only for the time the car is used. And both parties help to maximize the use of an idle car and contribute to the health of our environment.

"I Earn Cash for Grad School by Renting out My Car"

featuring Emmanuel Zamora, PhD student

Emmanuel is in grad school learning brain science to more quickly diagnose and treat his clients with traumatic brain injuries. Between a full course load and a 20-hour per week internship, he doesn't have time for a part-time job to help make ends meet.

Instead, Emmanuel rents his car on Getaround to help defray the costs of owning his 2009 Toyota Prius. About a year ago he found out about Getaround from a brochure left on his windshield, and decided to sign up for the service.

Since then, he has rented out his car more than 50 times and makes $300-400 a month in return for what he says "takes less than four hours per month" to respond to requests, clean his car, and make sure it's always gassed up. Emmanuel was able to pay off his car much sooner than he anticipated, so now he can use the extra cash to stay ahead of his bills.

In more than a year of renting out his car, the worst thing that happened was a driver who parked the car badly, left the ignition on hybrid power, and didn't lock the doors. Fortunately, nothing bad happened and Emmanuel wasn't soured by the experience. "I just probably wouldn't rent to her again," he said.

There are also pleasant surprises. "A woman who rents my car works at the San Francisco Chocolate Factory. Every time she uses my car, she leaves me a little box of chocolates. And another woman left a six-pack of ginger ale on my front seat. I first thought she'd inadvertently left it, but she wrote me a message saying it was a gift." Sweet.

How to Take a Free Road Trip

Type of Exchange	Sharing Components
Rent	Underutilized Resource
	Peer to peer
	Make money

It's an age-old question for people without cars: How to get from A to B quickly, cheaply, and safely? Hitchhiking used to be an accepted way of getting free rides, but these days it can be considered downright dangerous. You can try to bum rides from your friends, but everyone is just so busy! And what if you need a ride to somewhere 200 miles away? Craigslist.com is one of the oldest ways to share rides and it works well, but the people using that internet service are anonymous. In this section, we'll show you the new wave of "hitching it" by using the internet to match up rides with riders, all of whom can be reference-checked and A-OK'd beforehand.

Some of the best places to find shared rides are big cities and college campuses. Services like Zimride.com connect with Facebook and give you the names and faces of your fellow travelers, complete with reviews, and a payment system to share costs. And old standby Craigslist is still worth checking out.

For example, if you're heading to Los Angeles from San Francisco there are many rides leaving every day. If you're somewhat flexible about your departure and return times you can usually find a ride for half the price of a bus ticket and significantly less than you'd spend flying. Plus, you might make new friends along the way, or at the very worst end up with another "only in California" story for your autobiography.

If you drive long distances, stop throwing money away and fill up those empty seats. Every open seat in your car could help someone get where they need to go and earn you a few bucks.

Ok then, let's buckle our seat belts!

HOW TO TAKE A FREE ROAD TRIP

Say you're planning on going up to see your family in Portland, OR, during Thanksgiving time and you're leaving from San Francisco, CA. You can either drive alone and find yourself muttering back at the talk-radio shows on those long stretches, or you can charge passengers $50 per seat each way and make the trip into a one-of-a-kind experience while helping other people get to their own turkey-day dinners.

STEP 1: Confirm Your Trip

Before you can offer, like, any rides, you must have some details firmed up, such as where you're headed and when you're leaving. Once you're locked in, then you can post the ride and start getting people signed up.

STEP 2: Map Your Trip

If you'll be passing through other cities along the way, also post your trip in those locations as possible pickup and drop-off points. This gives you more options and could appeal to more riders.

STEP 3: Post Your Ride

Decide on a ridesharing site and post the ride:

- ► Craigslist.org – see "rideshare" in "community" –you can also use a search Zimride.com – largest U.S. site offers Facebook login for verification, has user profiles, handles payments, allows for recommendations
- ► Ridejoy.com – uses Facebook for verification, payments are up to drivers

To get the best response, it's usually best to post the rideshare at least two to three days in advance. And if you end up posting on Craigslist, you might want to delete and repost your ad the day you're leaving to catch any last-minute riders and fill any open seats.

In your post, be clear about:

- ► Departure time
- ► Pickup point(s)
- ► Cost per seat

- ► Luggage space
- ► Locations along with way
- ► Drop-off point(s)
- ► Information about you: age, profession, interests
- ► Expectations and rules – smoking, eating, music, pit-stops, etc.

Note that even if you don't need the money, you can still take passengers for free and do a good thing for others and our environment.

STEP 4: Check Out the Rider(s)

Get the riders' first and last names and make sure that you have enough information to Google them. Also chat with each person on the phone and check out their vibes. If anything feels off, trust your instincts and look for other riders. You can politely let them know you've had an overwhelming response and will not be able to give them a ride this time.

STEP 5: Confirm the Riders

If you're using Craigslist, you can call each rider and confirm the pickup time, pickup location, and drop-off point. If you're using Zimride, you can confirm the ride by having the rider book the trip on Zimride.com.

To seal the deal, make sure all riders agree on the price – it's a business deal, and you don't want a rider thinking they can just offer you a joint to get the ride.

STEP 6: Begin the Trip!

Pick up the rider(s) as previously discussed:

Be on Time

This should go without saying, but be courteous and keep your word all the way through the ride. Remember, the rider isn't a friend who knows you, so do your best to put them at ease.

Try to Choose One Pickup Spot

If you're picking up multiple people from the same city, try to choose one central transit point to avoid running all over town. And be specific – don't just say "Civic Center," but avoid ambiguity by adding "the northwest corner of Grove and 8th Street, in front of the Carl's Jr." Choosing a location that's convenient for people to wait is good form as well.

Know How to Identify Your Riders

Hopefully, you've seen what they look like on Google or Facebook and also gotten a general physical description of each person during your phone chats. Have their cellphone numbers handy in case you can't easily find them.

STEP 7: Enjoy the Drive

Keep the music neutral.

Just because you're a metal fan doesn't mean your riders are. Consider having an auxiliary cable or a USB hookup for music so that your riders can share their music with you and vice versa. Also note that loud music will make conversation difficult.

Agree on Food and Pit Stops

Set the tone at the beginning by saying how often and where you're planning to stop for food and gas. Most riders are fairly flexible, but you should be willing to make adjustments depending on your riders' needs.

Follow the Riders' Vibes

Some people are talkers and some aren't, and some riders may just sleep or listen to their own music on headsets. Some conversations may begin organically as the ride progresses and people adjust to the rhythm of the road.

Be Fun

For those folks who are into a shared experience, ask questions, discuss current events, or play car games and get to know your fellow passengers. These all may help pass the time and, who knows, you might even make some new friends.

STEP 8: Drop off the Rider(s)

The drop-off locations should have been agreed upon up front. Even if you've chosen public transit points, however, you may want to take riders to their final destinations as a courtesy. It helps if your car or phone have GPS capabilities.

When you drop off your rider(s), offer to help them with their luggage and/or wait that extra minute to make sure they get inside okay, especially at night.

STEP 9: Reflect on the Experience

After you complete the rideshare, you'll probably have a lot to think about, especially if you've enjoyed having some all-too-rare leisurely and meaningful conversations. Consider what you've learned, how much money you saved, how you helped people, and perhaps how quickly the ride time passed. Perhaps ridesharing will become something you'll do regularly?

How to "Hitchhike" Safely

Type of Exchange	Sharing Components
Rent	 Underutilized Resource
	Peer to peer
	Save money

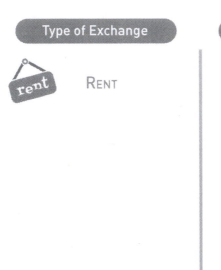

STEP 1: Join Up

In metropolitan or high-commute areas you may have several options for joining ridesharing and local carpooling services. For rideshares (mostly long distances), check out Zimride.com and Ridejoy.com.

In your city or town, you might also look for existing car pool or van pool setups. For example, in the Bay Area there is an ad hoc service called Casual Carpool where drivers can pick up riders at prescribed points to and from the East Bay and San Francisco. The riders can chip in for bridge tolls and this greatly helps reduce the traffic backups on the bridges.

Commuter parking lots just off the freeways make it easy for carpooling groups to form and function. You can also check membership services like Carpooling.com to offer and request rides, where monies change hands electronically. Note that by adding more people, the vehicle should qualify to use any carpool lanes which, in some metropolitan areas, could get you to and from work way faster.

If you're a student or faculty member at a college or university, check with Student Relations to see if there is a ridesharing network already set up. Zimride has such a system at over 125 universities across the U.S.

STEP 2: Look for Rides

Do searches on both Craigslist and Zimride to find ride offers that match your timetable and destination. Note that if you're going on a long trip, say cross-country, you may need to plan your trip in stages and choose major cities and hubs where you can get connections to your final destination.

Once you find a ride that looks good, send a message to the driver. As rides are often offered at the last minute, it's best to call the driver as well. Cars often fill up quickly and riders sometimes bail out as the time approaches, so calling the driver is definitely advisable.

Just as drivers should vet their passengers, make sure you check out the driver on Google, Facebook, and other social media to make sure they're someone you'd like to ride with, i.e. they have a job, friends, an online reputation, etc.

STEP 3: Create a "Ride Wanted" Ad

If you've exhausted the searching options and still haven't found your ride, try posting an ad on Craigslist starting with "ride wanted" so drivers can find you. If you use Zimride.com, select "post a ride" and then "passenger only." Note that Zimride also lists a suggested contribution, which can be adjusted.

In your ride wanted ad, include:

- ▶ Date/time you want to leave (and/or return)
- ▶ Your general location for pickup
- ▶ Your exact location for drop-off
- ▶ Relevant details about you, your interests, your luggage, etc.
- ▶ How much you're willing to pay for ride
- ▶ Contact phone number

It's up to you how much information you're willing to share, but the details about who you are could be as simple as "29, female, live in Los Angeles, working on Masters degree in Art History." You don't have to provide a life story or even a last name – just enough to give people an idea of what you're like in person.

STEP 4: Vet the Driver

This means:

- ▶ Google, Facebook, et al, them
- ▶ Talk to them by phone
- ▶ Make sure the trip details are clear and complete
- ▶ Trust your instincts

If the driver doesn't have a sufficient online presence, then you probably don't have any business hopping into a car with them. While talking to the driver by phone, make sure you listen to your inner voice. Sharing a ride isn't worth risking your safety, so if something seems weird, it probably is. And if you're female and only feel comfortable getting rides from women, then it's perfectly okay to just search for women drivers.

STEP 5: Request a Seat

You request a seat in the driver's car once you decide that they're the ride you want to take. They then have a given time period in which to accept this request. If you want to speed it along, feel free to email or otherwise contact them and let them know you're interested. Another helpful feature of Zimride is the driver's response time. If you see that they have an abysmal response time and you're in a rush to get on the road then maybe you should request a ride from another driver.

STEP 6: Confirm the Details

Things change, so make sure you reiterate the important things like pickup time, route, expected drop off time, drop off location and how to pay before the actual pick up just so there's no confusion.

STEP 7: Pay the Driver

If you use Zimride.com you pre-pay for the ride online. If you use a more informal service such as Craigslist, you should probably pay the driver when you are picked up. That way there is no awkward energy around payments. Always have exact cash on hand.

STEP 8: Thank the Driver

To show your appreciation and keep people motivated to offer rides, thank your driver after the ride with a quick email or by SMS text message. Some sites also have options for posting recommendations online. If so, do that as well.

HOW TO DITCH YOUR CAR USING THE SHARING ECONOMY

When you participate in Shareable Transportation, you literally have a new fleet of options at your feet. You can rent a convertible to impress your date, rent a truck to move that sofa, or rent a hybrid to drive a long distance. Plus, you can use public transit, car pools, rideshares, and car shares to get around and save money.

How much money? Well, owning a mid-sized car in the U.S. costs an average of $8,487 per year and, for city dwellers, that doesn't even include parking. That's over $700 per month! Every month!

Now imagine how far that money could go using transport on demand. If you need a taxi or a ride share, grab one. Need to take a short trip? Hop on public transit or take your bike. Have to do some errands? Utilize a car share. Need to get out of town? Check out ridesharing possibilities.

STEP 1: Educate Yourself

Use the web to find out what's available in your area. Ask your nomad friends how they manage to get around. Be creative and consider low-tech options like walking and bike riding. Learn about public transportation, carpooling, and commuter options. Find out how to rent cars or buy rides from your neighbors.

Learn about ridesharing for longer trips. And be sure to download all relevant smartphone apps to have all the information right at your fingertips. Think "lean and green" in the steps below, en route to your new Shareable Transportation lifestyle.

STEP 2: Research Public Transit

To whatever degree possible, use existing public transportation options. Note that most metro systems have many types of discount cards for students, seniors, commuters, etc. Use sites like Hopstop.com to find transit routes, maps, directions, and schedules.

STEP 3: Use Peer-to-Peer Ridesharing

Sidecar, Uber, and Lyft are peer-to-peer ridesharing services where "civilian" drivers are paid to get riders from from Point-A to Point-B in their own car. The entire transaction is handled by an app on your smartphone – you can book the ride, track the approaching car, and pay for the ride using the same interface. The best part? You can get picked up wherever you are and dropped at whatever location you want. No more waiting around in the rain trying to hail a taxi! And now, all of these services are experimenting with "shared rides" so that you can share a ride (and the expense) with a person being picked up from roughly the same area as you, and being dropped off in a similar location.

STEP 4: Rent a Car

When you need a car, rent one from a peer-to-peer network like Getaround or Relayrides. You'll quickly be able to find your desired vehicle, and probably from someone right in your neighborhood. Go to the website and shop around for the best price, coolest wheels, and most convenient pickup location.

STEP 5: Use Ridesharing

If you're headed out of town on a road trip that involves some distance, consider using ridesharing sites to find drivers who are heading the same way. To find these services, use Zimride.com, Ridejoy.com, or good ol' Craigslist.org (under "rideshare" in the "community" section).

STEP 6: Ditch Your Wheels!

Once you've got your transportation needs completely handled by these various services, you can then take that final step and become car-free and carefree. You can sell your car on Craigslist, donate it to a worthwhile charity (and get a tax write-off), give your wheels to a friend in need, or enter your no-longer-needed mobile in a demolition derby. Congratulations, you have taken one giant leap for mankind into the new Shareable Transportation economy!

STEP 7: Find Ways to Use All Your Extra Money

Oh, let me count the ways! Or heck, put it in the bank and save for something really worthwhile. Ha-ha, just a thought.

THE FUTURE OF SHAREABLE TRANSPORTATION

The "science fiction" future of personal transportation is already here, idling out at a curb near you, with the emergence and growing acceptance of self-driving cars. New models could eventually have sharing capabilities built in. Just think, a car so smart that it knows your patterns and current calendar well enough to predict when it will be sitting idle, and thus advertise itself for rentals..

Parking may not be sexy, but it is nevertheless expensive. The cost of a parking spot to call your own is skyrocketing up to $300 per month or more in some cities. Today, neighbors are turning their under-utilized driveways and garages into cash. If you insist on having a car you'd best have a place to put it, especially in cities like San Francisco which is rumored to have something like 100,000 more cars than street parking spaces.

Currently peer-to-peer services like Sidecar, Uber, and Lyft make it possible to get a ride across town with the help of a registered driver, or new friend, as the case may be. These services work via a smartphone app that map your current location and destination, and then push your request out to nearby drivers, giving you ride options within seconds. Best of all? Now, with with all of these peer-to-peer ridesharing services, there is an option for shareable rides, where you split the cost of a ride with someone nearby headed to a similar destination. Talk about disrupting the expensive and often unresponsive taxi industry!

These ridesharing services are so easy, available, and addictive that owning a car is beginning to seem superfluous in more and more urban areas. If you know you can always get a quick and economical ride across town at any time just by using your smartphone, why do you need a car? These peer-to-peer ridesharing services are currently operating in many locations and will soon be expanding into many other cities across the U.S. and the world.

If you do happen to have a car and you head out of a major airport on a trip, look no further than flightcar.com for free parking, a car wash, and cash every time your car is rented out while you're away.

And what about other vehicles like planes, boats, RVs, and motorhomes? If you have a group of friends who would like to co-own and share these types of fun vehicles, there is sharezen.com, which manages the sharing of operating costs as well as the scheduling, maintenance, usage, and all other aspects of the shared resource. Try boatbound.com for peer-to-peer boat rentals and rvshare.com for RVs.

Okay, enough about motorized vehicles already. What about bicycles? While bike shares are everywhere in Paris and New York, many cities have yet to catch up with this emerging phenomenon. In a bike share, bicycles are made available and returnable in convenient areas where hourly, daily, or weekly rentals can be made either free or by low-cost, member-based, or IT-based transactions. Spinlister.com can also help you rent or rent out a bike.

The bottom line is that the personal transportation space, especially in cities, is changing rapidly as new technologies and modalities come online. This is a good thing, especially as densely-packed urban centers are trying to limit traffic congestion and create better living environments.

Shareable Work

"What happens when work is no longer a place, but a state of mind? When the trappings that have defined the economy as we knew it are stripped away and we start from the bare essence of what it means to make a living?"

-Jeremy Neuner
Founder of NextSpace Coworking
Author of The Rise of the Naked Economy

A recent study by Rutgers University showed that, of all college graduates since 2006, only a little over half have a full-time job and 11% have no job at all. This is particularly shocking and almost counterintuitive. After all, a college degree is supposed to be your key to financial stability, right? Unfortunately, in the midst of a global recession jobs continue to be in short supply, regardless of your qualifications.

So what is a person to do? Continue sending out dozens, or even hundreds of resumes, cover letters, and applications in return for no response? Take that job at the fast-food place while you finish your screenplay? Play the lottery? Unfortunately, many highly-educated people have either quit looking for work altogether or settled for part-time work far below their grade level. Do you want fries with that?

So we're happy to introduce you to the world of Shareable Work to help you find work that empowers you, supports you financially, fits into your schedule, and enables you to control your destiny. Even during these rough economic times Shareable Work can give you an economic foot up to pay off debt, afford that vacation, or keep you afloat while you're building a new business or finding the right career.

In this chapter we'll show you how to adapt to these changing times and find work to fulfill your dreams and create your most excellent future. And as you're on your way to that future, it's important to stay in the game – keep engaged, try new approaches, step outside your comfort zone, take advantage of opportunities no matter how small or even how unrelated to your ultimate goal. You never know where your next big break will come from.

HOW TO WORK FROM ANYWHERE

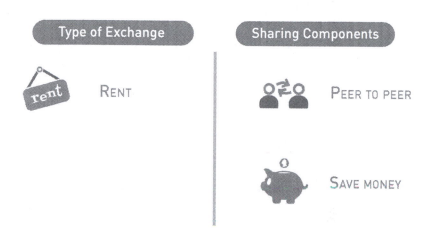

Type of Exchange	Sharing Components
RENT	PEER TO PEER
	SAVE MONEY

Converging trends in technology, economics, geography, and culture are creating new mashups for employment possibilities, making this an exciting time to be alive and, well, working.

Whether you fix computers, teach Pilates, or do web design, the internet is making it possible for you to translate your skills into the brave new world of work anywhere. You can fix computers over an iPhone app that taps into computers on the cloud, teach Pilates over Skype, or design websites in Bali for customers in Brooklyn.

That said, you don't have to become a wandering nomad, or quit your job, or seek enlightened work on a mountaintop. There are shareable resources at your fingertips that give you the information to change jobs, learn new skills, and choose the lifestyle you want. This guide will show you ways to lead a more flexible life where you can spend more time with family and friends, travel the world, and/or cowork in collaborative centers that boost your creativity and support your passions.

Working from anywhere brings up exciting, yet daunting, dilemmas and quandaries.

How you tackle these questions depends on your professional interests, financial situation, core values, and life stage. Reflect on ways you can apply your current skill set and knowledge base to generate work over the internet. You'll need to be creative and think outside the cubicle.

As Jeremiah Owyang, a collaborative economy expert and the founder of Crowd Companies says, "In the future, the established workplace won't just be within four walls, but available, anywhere, and on-demand."

"How can I work from anywhere?"

If you decide to become your own boss, you get to call the shots on where, when, and how much you work. The sharing economy has mighty big shoulders and can help you realize your goals, live your dreams, and reach new professional or creative heights (see sections on Kickstarter, Udemy, and Skillshare). For example, consider using crowdfunding to get the cash you need to fund your ideas. Use the internet to learn new skills to get you on the road to joining the independent workforce.

Did you know that freelancers constitute more than 30% of the U.S. workforce, comprising 45 million people? And there's plenty of room for one more.

"But I my job! I just want more flexibility"

According to Forrester Research, 375 million people worldwide currently have the luxury of working remotely. And the trend is growing. For example, large corporations like Hewlett Packard are making 40% of their employees remote in order to more quickly respond to changing conditions and cut down on operating overhead. So, don't get discouraged if your current workspace is in the middle of a soulless cube farm.

Being a remote worker doesn't always mean traveling the world and drinking Mai Tai's on the beach. You can still work from home, or a coworking space (more on this later), or a neighborhood coffee shop, or a mix of all three. Again, the idea is to create the work environment that works for you. And if that means a deck chair on a tropical beach somewhere, then so be it.

In any case, as we move further into the volatile 21st century new concepts, paradigms, and realities will continue to expand our current definitions of work, workers, and workplaces.

Work Styles Defined:

- ▶ Employee: works for an organization, usually in-house

- ▶ Remote Worker: has flexibility in scheduling and whereabouts; some get to work from home several days a week, while others are given permanent flexibility as long as they are performing

- ▶ Freelancer: bids on contracts or projects, wins them, and delivers results to clients. Typical freelancers do design, tech development, marketing, etc. If you're interested in joining this growing population, check out these resources: freelancer.com, odesk.com, and elance.com

- ▶ Entrepreneur: creates products or services that are marketed to consumers or other businesses. An entrepreneur includes everyone from artists who sell their creations to café owners to tech startup founders

► <u>Consultant:</u> usually established in their career and have previously worked as employees, freelancers, or entrepreneurs and now are contracted out to provide skilled work or direction to companies and individuals. Note that they are sometimes also called contractors.

You'll want to be aware of which style of worker you are for tax purposes, as the I.R.S. has specific guidelines for determining, say, when a worker is considered an employee vs. a consultant, contractor, or freelancer. It matters too about whether you receive a W-2, 1099, or other statement of your earnings. Before tax time, you'll want to talk with an accountant to make sure you're doing all the right stuff.

How Andrew Took His Business to the Next Level by Trading Spaces
Swapyourshop.com Case Study

Andrew Zarick needed some new stimulation. Though New York City still remained vibrant and interesting, his work had become stagnant. "After three years in a marketing firm, things get stale," he lamented. Funny enough, Andrew's boss sent him the URL to swapyourshop.com which enables a worker to "swap" with another worker somewhere else. The workers trade living spaces for weeks or months, with each worker still doing his old job, but now remotely from the swapped worker's workspace.

Unbeknownst to his boss, Andrew took Swapyourshop seriously. He quickly fired off a few messages to fellow marketers in the Netherlands and Mexico. One day a message arrived from a guy named Jose in Valencia, Spain.

Valencia wasn't originally on Andrew's radar, but he decided to check it out because Jose was so insistent on coming to NYC. After a month of Skype interactions, Andrew and Jose struck a deal to swap shops and living spaces. Andrew then had to convince his boss that this would be a great way to: continue doing his job remotely, retain him as an employee, and enable him to bring back marketing ideas from Europe. And that having Jose working from Andrew's cubicle would benefit the company as well.

Finally, with his boss's blessing, Andrew hopped on a plane to Valencia, Spain. He was able to spend a couple of days with Jose who introduced him around to his English-speaking friends. By the time Jose left for New York, Andrew's phone was loaded up with numbers of new Spanish contacts.

"The experience was really intimate," Andrew said later. "When you live in someone else's space and they live in yours, you get an idea of the other person and how they interact with your personal space. It's definitely different from an Airbnb rental because of how it's positioned as a professional experience instead of just travel."

Since the six-week swap, Andrew has been back to Valencia twice and he communicates with his new Spanish friends on a weekly basis.

And there is an amazing postscript to the story. In 2009 Andrew co-founded a creative business community called Digital DUMBO (Down Under the Manhattan Bridge Overpass) which regularly attracts over 800 attendees to their monthly technology-centric events. He had envisioned taking Digital DUMBO international, but lacked the resources to pull it off. Swapyourshop created a serendipitous bridge between Andrew and Jose to make that a reality. Digital DUMBO has now expanded from Brooklyn to Boston, Dallas, London, and, you guessed it, Valencia.

How to Share Office Space by Coworking

Coworking is a global trend where entrepreneurs, freelancers, consultants, and remote workers all share office space in a community-oriented environment. This enables independent workers in often different disciplines to escape the isolation of working alone, and to create opportunities for those synergistic, paradigm-shifting conversations around the water cooler.

Most coworking spaces have an open floor plan that makes collaboration easy. There are usually offices, desks, tables, and even couches, as well as "hot desks" which can be shared between several individuals at different times. There is often a café-like setting where members can come in, tap into the wi-fi, and work for the day or by the month. As the emphasis is generally on community, these spaces also schedule social events, trainings, and mixers to encourage people to talk to each other and interact on a regular basis.

The Benefits of Coworking

There are multiple ways that coworking adds personal and professional value above and beyond just working from home or from your local Starbucks.

Access to the Community

When you work in a shared space, you get the benefits of being around other people. This proximity allows you to make connections, get feedback on ideas, bid on projects together, refer clients, and make new friends. For solo-preneurs and freelancers, just being around other creative people can be motivating. Fun, even.

Physical Mailing Address

If you work from home, you probably don't want to use your home address for privacy reasons. Also, your home address probably doesn't send the same message of stability and success that a metropolitan office address with a suite number does. Find a coworking space with an address close to the city center so that your Google My Business listing comes up higher in results for searches like "Tax Accountant San Francisco."

Tip: Even if you don't want to work at a coworking space, buy a mailbox membership to use their address.

Meeting Space

Most coworking memberships come with at least a few hours of bookable time in an onsite meeting room. You will typically have to reserve this space at least a day in advance. This is a great benefit for holding meetings, talks, presentations, and even social events.

Separate Work from Home

Of course coworking provides a space for you to work, but the real juice is having a place that's separate from your living environment. (Besides, working alone sucks!)

Wi-Fi and Utilities

If you've ever made the rounds of neighborhood coffee shops, you know that trying to find a clean well-lighted place with free wi-fi and tolerable music can be maddening. Besides, downing all those lattes with triple shots can put a serious crimp in your budget. With coworking, all of your utilities are covered in your membership fees.

Coffee and Printer

Since many people in the know migrate from coffee shops to coworking spaces, one of the near-universal perks of coworking communities is free coffee. Depending on the space, you may even get copies included with your membership. Either way, having access to a high-quality printer capable of large runs is useful. If you're on a roll, do you want to break your concentration by having to run out to a copy shop? Or coffee shop?

Events and Event Space

As a member, you'll get invited to members-only coworking events where you can mix and mingle with other members and maybe even pick up some new skills at informational sessions. And if you ever need to hold an event of your own for your business, club, or organization, you can usually rent the space in the evenings or on weekends.

Work Better

According to the First Global Coworking Survey conducted by Deskmag of 661 members in 24 countries, these advantages were cited by coworkers:

- ▶ 85% were more motivated
- ▶ 90% enjoyed interactions with coworkers
- ▶ 60% organized their workdays more efficiently
- ▶ 42% reported higher earnings

Membership Types and Typical Costs:

There are multiple options for membership at most coworking sites and, depending on your city and country, your mileage may vary, as they say.

So consider the terminology and costs below as just general guidelines:

Daily – up to $25/day

Swing in for the day. Great for the traveling professional or the freelancer who may only need to host the occasional client meeting in a spiffy professional environment. You usually won't get much more than just access to the common spaces or communal desks. The drawback is that you you typically have to leave the premises at the end of business (so no late nights).

Café Membership – $100-400/month

This entry-level membership provides full coworking benefits, however it usually doesn't guarantee desk space, so you may end up working from a couch, an unoccupied desk, or a communal table.

Hot Desk – $200-400/month

This entitles you to a desk to work at, but it's not a permanent one. So you don't get to leave your stuff there because you may work from a different desk each time.

Permanent Desk – $200-600/month

You get a desk to call your own, and it may be in an office or a public area. You can leave your desktop computer, files, and supplies here if desired.

Private Office – $500+/month

This is the way to go if you make a lot of phone calls, especially of a confidential or proprietary nature. Plus you still get all the benefits of being in a community space.

HOW TO FIND A SHAREABLE WORKSPACE

STEP 1: Search for Spaces

Head over to Deskwanted.com, Desksnear.me or Liquidspace.com and type in your desired city. You can then browse locations by looking at the photos, learning about the amenities, and reviewing comments from others about the space.

STEP 2: Find the Right Space

Call ahead and see if it is cool for you to drop-in. Many coworking sites don't advertise this, but they are often happy to let you drop-in and check them out for the day (free). This is a great way to catch the vibes at the spaces you're most interested in.

Liquidspaceapp.com has built an iPhone/Android app that allows you to browse coworking spaces, meeting areas in business centers and hotels, and other public spaces where work could be done. You can browse locations and see which space best suits your needs for convenience, vibe, and price. And the beauty is, you can also see what times are available and book the space right in the app or on the website.

STEP 3: Or Find a Free Space

In many metropolitan areas, there are companies that offer a free communal space to work. Places like Wix in San Francisco (wixsf.com) offer free space to entrepreneurs. There are also the Capital One 360 Cafes (cafes.capitalone360.com), which are free meeting and work spaces in 7 major cities including: San Francisco, Los Angeles, Chicago, St. Cloud, Boston, New York, and Philadephia. It may not be total altruism, however, as they may expect you to talk them up and/or use their products.

Another emerging trend is subsidized coworking as part of an effort to economically revitalize certain areas. One such example is Las Vegas, NV, where Zappos founder Tony Hsieh has put $350 million into such efforts. At their 6th Street coworking location, members can drop in everyday for just $50 monthly.

If you travel, also check out Seats2meet.com, which is a network of coworking spaces (clustered mostly in the Netherlands, Germany, Belgium, and the United Kingdom), that offer a free coworking option for freelancers and entrepreneurs who are willing to share their skills.

STEP 4: Or Go Wi-Fi

If all else fails you can search for free wi-fi. If you have a smartphone, download the Free Wi-Fi Finder application for your iPhone or Android and find the closest place. Smart options include public libraries, museums, Starbucks, and McDonalds.

THE POWER OF COWORKING

featuring Nextspace.us
by Chelsea Rustrum

Four months into a coworking stint at Nextspace in Santa Cruz, CA, I witnessed firsthand the magic of "the spaces in between" and the inherent value of collaboration. To me, the spaces in between represent the intangible advantages of being in the same place at the same time with others, as well as the benefits of serendipitous interactions.

Sol Lipman, a serial entrepreneur and "idea man", hand-picked eight people from the 100 or so members at Nextspace and whisked them all off in an RV to a camp in Southern California where food and housing would be provided.

Up until then the group members had had very few ties with each other, besides the occasional "hello" in the hallway. But Sol had a vision. He'd chosen a group of ambitious, highly-skilled go-getters with the coworking spirit and gave them a structure, a cause, and an avenue for creation. The team worked 14+ hours a day building a location-based iPhone app similar to Foursquare, drank copious amount of beer at night, and were no doubt serenaded by Sol's breakout guitar sessions.

The near-strangers, now completely stoked, returned to Nextspace as a tight-knit group of friends sharing inside jokes. In just seven days the team had built an application called Rallyup, which gave people the ability to check-in with their location, text, and a photo to show their friends where they are. The app was built with a more robust design that gave users a richer experience than Foursquare.

After the trip, all eight of them moved out of their respective offices at NextSpace and into one giant bullpen where they could work side-by-side. The team fleshed out Rallyup for nine months, and then they and their application got bought out by AOL for a reported $10 million.

Sol came along with the team to AOL and negotiated awesome salaries, collaborative office space, and a new corporate authorization to continue developing cool new applications, only now with bigger budgets and corporate clout.

The Nextspace experience had an impact – professionally, personally, and financially – on every member of the group. They started out as individual freelancers and entrepreneurs and through their shared coworking experience grew into a rock star development team. Such is the power of coworking. And that's just one story.

THE TASKRABBIT STORY

Another option for Shareable Work is TaskRabbit.

Since the very framework of how TaskRabbit works has changed since the inception of writing this book, we thought we'd take this opportunity to talk about what TaskRabbit was - and why we considered it to be a part of the sharing economy, as well as how it's changed.

Taskrabbit.com is an online community-based service-networking site created to help people get tasks done by connecting them with other people willing to do the work. TaskRabbit originally provided a means for unemployed people, under-employed workers, students, stay-at-home moms, active retirees, and those with extra time to earn money, learn new skills, hone old skills, network in their community, and sometimes have fun little adventures.

The service connected TaskRabbits (workers approved by TaskRabbit) to help others de-clutter, de-stress, and generally de-complicate their lives. People would post tasks ranging from website help, to backyard landscaping, to a request for a bartender at their private party. TaskRabbits bid on the project and if the Rabbit was chosen, the person who posted the task or "Task-Poster" would communicate the logistic details needed to carry out their task. Once the task was complete, the TaskPoster would pay their TaskRabbit through the system.

Today, TaskRabbit no longer allows task bidding on a project basis and is more of an hourly service with a focus on cleaning, handyman, moving, and personal assistance help. Each TaskRabbit sets their hourly rate.

In addtion to TaskRabbit, there are other similar and interesting options that have emerged.

Loconomics.com

As one of the first of its kind - Loconomics is a member owned organization where the people who do the work will actually own a portion of the company, based on their contributions.

The service includes categories like: home, pet, child, personal, transportation, office, senior, and celebrations where you can post tasks and offer services.

Time Banks

Time Banking is a lot like TaskRabbit, only instead of transacting with money, participants utilize time dollars. Each hour is worth one time dollar, regardless of what type of work it is. You can post any type of offer or request, and someone from your community will complete the request. Head to the "How to Participate in a Local Time Bank" section to learn more about joining and participating in time banks.

How to Make Extra Money When You're Underemployed
Taskrabbit.com

Type of Exchange	Sharing Components
SELL	PEER TO PEER
	MAKE MONEY

How to Use Taskrabbit to Share Skills and Make Money!

Taskrabbit.com is currently operational in nearly 20 major cities and will soon be expanding into others. The service has an established client base and a growing reputation, making it easier for you to augment your income by completing tasks. A diligent and experienced TaskRabbit (AKA Tasker) can make $50-200 per day, depending on the market area and individual skill set.

So if you've got some spare time, like to help people, and have needed skills, then you too can become a TaskRabbit and use those extra bucks to pay down credit cards, upgrade your vacation, or buy that 8-track player on eBay.

Becoming a TaskRabbit (someone who does the work) is more involved than becoming a Task Poster (someone who needs work done). The service's vetting process makes sure that all TaskRabbits are qualified, responsible, and trustworthy, so that a consistent and high level of satisfaction is maintained.

You must be be 21 years or older and live in one of the major cities where TaskRabbit operates to qualify as a Tasker.

HOW TO BECOME A TASKRABBIT (TASKER) FOR FUN AND PROFIT

STEP 1: Create an Account

First you must signup, by clicking the "Sign up" button at the top of the homepage at Taskrabbit.com. Then click "I want to be a Tasker."

Enter the following:
Birthdate
Type of Phone
Address

The direct address for your application is: taskrabbit.com/apply

STEP 2: Take the Quiz

Answer the quiz questions (there should be 11 of them). The answers to these questions can all be found within the TaskRabbit guidebook.

You must answer all of the questions correctly in order to proceed. You will get a few chances to get everything right, so don't worry if you don't pass the first time.

STEP 3: Provide Information for Background Check

Fill out information, including:

First Name
Last Name
Birthdate
Gender
Phone Number
Social Security Number
Back Account Number
Routing Number

The information you've previously entered should be auto-filled here.

STEP 4: Pass a Background Check

Following the approval of your video interview, a background check will be conducted. The service does this to ensure a high level of personal responsibility, trust, and compatibility.

STEP 5: Watch Video About Tasker Tools

This 5 minute video will give you information about iOS/Android app that you can use to make your job as a Tasker more efficient.

STEP 6: Set Your Availabilities

When you click through to the next step after watching the video, you will be able to set the times that you're available (weekdays and time of day you can work) as well set a zone using an interactive map that shows where you're able to complete tasks. If you get stuck at any point, you can watch the video on this page for more information.

STEP 7: Fill Out More Profile Details

These are a few open ended questions that will get posted to your profile, so be sure to put some thought into your answers to ensure that you get as many jobs as possible.

What makes you a great addition to the TaskRabbit community?

What do you do when you're not tasking?

When I'm tasking I always make sure to...

Do you have a vehicle you'd be willing to use for tasks?

STEP 8: Set Your Hourly Rates

At this point, you can choose which types of tasks you're best suited and set your hourly rate for the task type. TaskRabbit will give you a recommended range based on the type of task, but you can choose any hourly rate you'd like. The task categories include things like: cleaning, website design, writing/editing, furniture assembly, etc. Since the main categories offered to customers on the homepage include cleaning, handyman, moving help, and personal assistant, it would be wise for you to choose these categories and offer competitive rates to start.

STEP 9: Upload Your Photo

Make sure you upload a photo that demonstrates a high level of professionalism and your winning personality!

STEP 10: Wait for Your Application to be Reviewed

Once you submit you application, you will receieve this message:

"Thanks for your interest in joining the TaskRabbit community! Your application to become a Tasker has been received. We review applications on a rolling basis and accept new members based on marketplace needs. You'll hear from us as soon as there is a fit for your skills and interests in our marketplace."

Tips for Being a Tasker:

<u>Total Costs</u> – Consider the time it will take to get there, the time needed to complete the task, your transportation costs, etc. You will be reimbursed only for expenses directly related to the task, such as the cost of the groceries you're picking up, but not for your bus ride or parking fees. When you set your hourly rate, take all of these factors into consideration.

<u>Understand the Task</u> – It's okay to ask questions of the Task-Poster before bidding, or provide qualifying comments before accepting the job.

<u>Accept Tasks Quickly</u> – Accept jobs quickly (within less than 30 minutes) so that the jobs are not redistributed.

<u>Know Your Limits</u> – Make sure that you reeeally know how to do the task. Neither you nor the Task Poster wants to see you sweating extra hours trying to figure it out. This will not earn you great reviews either.

STEP 11: Receive Notifications of Tasks

Once you are an approved Tasker, the TaskRabbit community will see your profile when they search for the types of tasks you have signed on to accomplish. The app (for iPhone and Android) is a really important part of this - you must have the app downloaded and respond to task requests within 30 minutes, otherwise your task will be made available to other taskers.

STEP 12: Confirm Details & The Task

After you receive a task request, confirm the details by asking any necessary clarifying questions and be sure that you know the exact date and time that the task will need to be completed. If you are confident in your ability to complete the task, hit the "Confirm Task" button. If there is any reason you don't feel comfortable or able to complete the task, simply hit the "Forfeit" button, which will pass the task on to other Taskers.

STEP 13: Show Up & Complete Work

On your way to the job, use the app to notify the customer that you're in route using the chat feature. Once you arrive, complete the work as assigned. If the amount of time will go over what was originally agreed upon, notify the customer as soon as possible. If you're able to complete the extra work, feel free to do so, but you can also call TaskRabbit and have another Tasker complete the job.

At the completion of the work, open your app again and hit the "I'm done" button. Once you do that, you can submit your hours for payment. If you had any expenses, enter the amount on this screen to get reimbursed.

STEP 14: Get Paid

TaskRabbit takes 20% of your hourly rate as a fee. So expect that you'll receive 80% of whatever amount is billed. After invoicing the customer in the previous step, the monies earned will hit your checking account within 3-4 business days.

STEP 15: Become a TaskRabbit Elite

Every month, TaskRabbit denotes TaskRabbits who have performed a lot of jobs with high ratings as part of the TaskRabbit Elite, which means you will get even more jobs and will show up more prominently in search results.

To be part of the TaskRabbit Elite, you can quality by:

- ► Being in the top 13% of Taskers by tasks closed over the last 90 days
- ► Completing 3 tasks within any category within the last 30 days
- ► Have zero policy violations in the last 90 days
- ► Earn a 97% or better positive rating overall

Tips for Ranking High as a TaskRabbit:

- ► Become part of the TaskRabbit Elite (see above)
- ► Get positive feedback and reviews consistently
- ► Complete tasks regularly
- ► Focus on categories like cleaning, moving, handyman work, and personal assistance

"THE RIGHT WORK AT THE RIGHT TIME"

Featuring Renee of San Francisco

After a year of clinical misdiagnoses, 50-year-old Renee of San Francisco was finally diagnosed with cancer and underwent two years of chemotherapy. During that time, she spent more and more time alone and eventually didn't even want to leave her home. Depressed, anxious, and worn down, Renee was not only battling cancer, she was also facing financial disaster.

Social Security and disability didn't even cover the cost of her rent, let alone food, utilities, and her other living expenses. Renee used to be a limo chauffeur and had 28 year's experience in customer service, but she wasn't able to work those jobs due to the chemo treatments.

When she was on the verge of hopelessness, a friend suggested Renee take a look at TaskRabbit. A few days later, Renee was signed up and got her first job – to act as a "human alarm clock". As she explained, "I woke up early and went to this woman's house every morning at 6 a.m. for five straight days to get her out of bed. She was a lawyer and needed help to get back on the right time zone." Interestingly enough, the human alarm clock job is a popular task.

Renee adds, "Another guy wanted me to bring him Burger King for breakfast every morning and talk to him. He was coming out of a depression and I really enjoyed helping him." Other jobs gave Renee a creative outlet for expression, such as when a major brand needed someone to dress up as a mad scientist in Union Square. "I really got into character," she recalls.

Today, Renee works 20-25 hours a week on TaskRabbit, working when she has the physical and mental ability keep up. She only bids on jobs that will earn her $20 an hour or more. She has not only found a new way to earn a living, but she has integrated back into society and feels like she is once again contributing. For more info: taskrabbit.com/renee-de-a.

Additional Notes:

TaskRabbit fits nicely within the framework of the sharing economy since the service allows TaskRabbits to use their under-utilized time and skills in exchange for much-needed moolah. On the flipside, Task Posters are able to hire neighbors to make their lives more efficient, their households more orderly, and their stress levels more manageable. Businesses can also use TaskRabbit for ad hoc jobs that would otherwise be too disruptive if employees had to be pulled away from their regular work to do them. All told, a big win-win-win.

OTHER OPTIONS FOR SHAREABLE WORK

In this chapter you've been shown some options for keeping busy by helping others as you generate a positive cash flow. Also discussed were ideas about working anywhere, collaborating, and joining a local coworking community.

If you are lucky enough to be a freelancer, Shareable Work is already a part of your lifestyle! However, if you're a stay-at-home parent, student, retiree, under-employed, or unemployed, using your spare time in creative ways can make you money, keep you active, connect you with people, and get you back in the game. Heck, even if you have a full-time job, you can still participate in smaller ways. Or learn new skills by utilizing free online educational resources and/or attending in-person workshops, as discussed in the Shareable Education chapter.

In addition to checking out the Shareable Work opportunities mentioned below, take a look at the Shareable Home, Shareable Education, Shareable Creativity, and Shareable Transportation chapters for more innovative ways to generate signifant income.

Shareable Work Opportunities:

oDesk.com

oDesk is a global marketplace for posting jobs and hiring contractors to work remotely. What's great about oDesk is that you can bid on projects that require technical skills like administrative support, customer service, tech writing, graphic design, software development, marketing, and more. Note that oDesk charges

10% of the final project cost for administration. Payments are made online.

<u>Lyft, Sidecar, Uber</u>

As mentioned in the Shareable Transportation section, there are ride sharing technology companies that allow anyone with a safe driving record, car insurance, and a vehicle to earn income in their spare time, driving other people around. Many of these drivers earn as much as $20-30+ per hour and have great flexiblity in terms of the hours and locations they are able to work. To learn more about these opportunies, visit: lyft.com, side.cr, and uber.com.

Fun Work Opportunities:

<u>Fivver.com</u>

Do quick jobs for people such as voice-overs and other easy, oftentimes fun and creative projects for $5 each. You won't get rich here, but it can be a fun way to pass time while earning some pocket money. Who knows, maybe you'll get your foot in the door somewhere by helping the right person.

<u>Gigwalk.com</u>

Gigwalk is great for anyone who has a smartphone, as many of the jobs require being on the ground to interview people, take photos, mystery shop, etc. Most jobs on Gigwalk are simple and only require a bit of work, but you can earn as much as $15-20 per hour.

Shareable Home

"Value unused = waste."

-Lisa Gansky
Author of The Mesh

Want to live rent-free? Or live in a rockstar mansion with your best friends? Maybe earn cash from unused space in your garage or driveway? You can, if you're ready to lead a more shareable lifestyle.

Just think, the next time you travel you could rent out your place while you're away. This not only allows you to travel longer and/or more often, but adds new options for your own accommodations while you're on the road. Plus, if you have a flexible work style as outlined in the Shareable Work chapter, you can travel the world for extended periods, all the while making serious money renting out your place and knowing you can return to your home base whenever you choose.

For short-term money making possibilities, you can host guests on Airbnb.com, allowing people from all around the world to stay in your home. Airbnb is a similar cultural exchange to Couchsurfing (couchsurfing.org) as discussed earlier in Shareable Travel, except that Airbnb guests pay you for their stay. Airbnb allows you to rent out your couch, an extra bedroom, your entire house, or your RV in the driveway. This helps fulfill a main Airbnb goal of enabling people to "travel like a human" by offering comfortable and personalized alternatives to white-walled hotel rooms.

And for other shareable economy options, think outside the home and consider renting out your driveway or garage – or even sharing an entire house with others through a coliving arrangement. In this chapter, we'll show you how you too can win the Shareable Home trifecta – living rent-free, living more communally, and/or sharing unused space. Hey, maybe even all of the above!

How to Live Rent-Free by Hosting Guests

Airbnb.com

Type of Exchange		Sharing Components	
rent	Rent	(bag)	Underutilized Resource
		(peer icon)	Peer to peer
		(wheelbarrow)	Make money

You can get paid while you travel, earn extra income while you're home, and maximize usage of your living space all by using Airbnb. The airbnb.com service makes for a classic win-win situation – guests save money because most rentals are cheaper than most hotels, and hosts make money by providing unused or underutilized living space.

STEP 1: Decide What to Rent

You can list your couch, spare room, apartment, home, in-law or rental unit, villa, etc. If you don't have a traditional sleeping space like a futon or a spare room, get creative and rent a spot in your back yard to campers. In expensive locales some travelers will be happy to pay for even a mat on the floor. And consider those times when you're not going to be home. You can maximize your rental dollars by listing your whole house.

If you live in a desirable destination city (especially if you're centrally located), you're sitting pretty for getting lucrative rentals. Cities are often over-booked during holidays, celebrations, festivals, conferences, sporting events, and the like. For example, in a heavily-visited city like San Francisco there will always be people seeking alternatives to the expensive, big-name hotels.

Even if you're not living in a big city, you can still be a hit. Airbnb is expanding and, if you're one of the first hosts in your town, your listing will stand out. Getting in early will get you more reviews which will cause your listing to rank higher in guest searches. People like to stay with interesting people and if your accommodations are also unique, appealing, and economical, then they will beat a path to your door.

STEP 2: List Your Space

Go to (airbnb.com). Next click on "List Your Space" Once you choose all of the options such as: home type, room type, number of people your space accomodates, and city - you'll be asked to sign up.

Connect with Facebook, Google, or an Email Address

This will allow you to grab details such as your profile picture, hobbies, and interests in one click. If you don't have Facebook or Google, you can still signup easily using the Sign up with Email option.

Think Up a Creative Title

First impressions matter. You want to pique curiosity and draw people in for a closer look at your space.

Write a Poetic Description

Unleash your inner Emily Dickinson and let your personality shine through when providing the relevant details. To mix a metaphor, it's the sizzle not the steak, yes? People respond best to short, witty copy that's easily scanned.

Tip: You can encourage potential guests to contact you for more information if they're undecided. Getting a dialog started is a great way to develop trust and build interest.

Take Good Photos

Make sure your pictures are high quality and show the entire space with all its amenities. Shoot from different angles to accentuate the positive.

Tip: You can request an Airbnb staff photographer to come onsite and take professional-quality photos – it's free! Hosts with professionally photographed places, they say, get twice as many bookings: (airbnb.com/photography).

Include Your Neighborhood

Be sure to specify the neighborhood you're in, so your listing will display for geographic searches by neighborhood.

Create Your Personal Profile

Add a high-quality photo or two and a snappy description of yourself. To some guests, <u>who</u> they're renting from may be as important as <u>what</u> they're renting. Ask your friends to recommend you to enhance your trust profile (see Step 4 below).

Tip: You may consider adding information to allow a potential guest to Google you or find you on social media sites like Linkedin. You can include the name of your blog, clubs, sports, associations, your job, business, etc. to give people the extra assurance that you're a trustworthy sort.

Tip: You can even make a 30-second intro video, which will show up where your profile photo is. When someone clicks the play button, they'll see you expounding enthusiastically about yourself and your place.

STEP 3: Set Price and Availability

Check the Market

When you first start out, check the rates for average-priced hotels and search Airbnb listings in your area for similar accommodations. Set your initial price low (perhaps 25% below your ideal rate) to lure in new guests. As you begin getting favorable reviews you can gradually raise your rates to market prices or even above if you're extra awesome. Airbnb can also guide you by using their pricing tool at: (airbnb.com/whats-my-place-worth).

Tip: Do you have last minute availability? Make a special offer to standbys at (airbnb.com/hosting/standbys). You can also sign up there to get standby request alerts by email.

Charge for Extra People

You can charge up to $10-25 per person per night for extra guests. Typically the first two guests are included if you're renting an entire apartment or a house.

Cleaning Fees

To charge or not to charge, that is the question. It's up to you, but charging does bring in more income. And it's a fee that people are used to paying with vacation rentals. Try to keep the fee reasonable, though, so you stay competitive.

You could also roll the cleaning fee into the cost per night, and mention that you don't charge a cleaning fee, but fully expect guests to be responsible and leave the place the way they found it.

Decide When to Rent

Set the availability calendar according to your situation. If you're going to be gone for a week in November, you could create a listing for your whole apartment for that week. Are you going to be around in December and feel like company? Change your spare bedroom or couch listing to reflect that.

Tip: Update your calendar frequently to reflect your schedule changes. Then you won't have to be responding to queries that conflict with your availability.

Tip: Try to attract short stays at first in order to get enough reviews to get ranked higher.

STEP 4: Enhance Your Trust Level

Request References from Friends

When you sign up for Airbnb and use Facebook to connect, you can see which Facebook friends are already on Airbnb. Shoot those peeps a message and ask them to review you here: (airbnb.com/users/references).

Connect Your Social Networks

To verify that you're a solid citizen and that other people like you, connect your account to Twitter, Facebook, and Linkedin to show potential guests how many social connections you have.

Add Your Phone Number

This further verification is good for three reasons: you can get text messages about new reservation requests, it adds an additional stamp of approval to your account, and your listing will rank higher.

STEP 5: Promote Your Listing

Post to Facebook

Share your Airbnb URL on Facebook to let your network know about your digs.

Tell Family and Friends

Send out an email to your family, friends, coworkers, team-mates, colleagues, and neighbors with the URL to your listing, alerting them that you're now accepting guests and you'd be much obliged if they refer people to you.

STEP 6: Respond to Inquiries ASAP

Respond to All Messages

Even if you get a message in a foreign language, always respond within 24 hours. Your response rate is used in the search algorithm to rank your listing. If someone messages you with an incomplete account, ask them to fill out their profile to give you more information about them.

Use your own set of standards to evaluate requests. You can politely decline any guest for any reason, but perhaps the best way is just to say that you're already working out the details with another guest for that period.

Get the Mobile App

The quicker you respond to requests, the more confirmations you'll get. So turn on text alerts on the app. Guests are often shooting off multiple requests and many will book with the quickest response. Plus, the more consistently you respond to all messages, the higher your search ranking will be.

STEP 7: Accept a Request

Only Accept Requests You Want

There is no Airbnb penalty for denying requests.

Only Accept Requests You Can Keep

This falls into the "no-brainer" category. Even if the guest has agreed to an iffy reservation, when you cancel a request it will negatively affect your listing.

Write a Welcome Email Template

Create a standard reply to tell your guest all relevant information like check-in/check-out times, your phone/email, and any other important facts. Make sure you ask for their expected check-in information, cellphone number, and answer any questions they might have.

Be as accommodating as you can about meeting up, giving them your keys, showing them around your place, etc. This is probably best accomplished by modifying your standard email template for each guest.

STEP 8: Be an Unforgettable Host

Make Sure Your Place Is Spotless

Even if you're just renting your futon, clean your kitchen and bathroom, and have the living area free of clutter. It's good form to provide clean towels and sheets, and you'll score bonus points for providing items like a coffee maker, hair dryer, clothes iron, wi-fi, etc.

Meet and Greet Your Guest

Welcome them into your home as a new friend. You'll both benefit from having a "house manual" that explains how everything works (wi-fi code, TV, washing machine, etc.). Also advisable is a list of "house rules" (no smoking, quiet hour times, etc.). Do what you can to make them feel comfortable, especially if they've had a long travel day.

Tip: Also provide a local "guidebook" of your neighborhood which might include public transit information, local sites of interest, tourist maps, etc.

Tip: If you can't be there in person, perhaps you could arrange for a TaskRabbit to greet your guest, and even clean your place beforehand.

Tip: Make sure you provide an emergency contact in case you are unavailable or your guest loses a key, etc.

Do Something Unique

If you're getting along with your guest, invite them to a business gathering, introduce them to your friends, offer them a ride, etc. If you're making an omelet, offer your guest one too. It's the little things that mean a lot.

STEP 9: Review Your Guest

The best way to get great, descriptive reviews is to write a stellar review for your guest immediately after their stay. That way, they will feel inclined to reciprocate.

Additional Airbnb Information:

Fees

Note that listing your space is free, but Airbnb will charge the host 3% of the rental fee after the stay. They will also charge the guest a service fee. Also note that the host can require a security deposit and a cleaning fee, if so desired.

Taxes

Make sure you comply with local laws. Some municipalities may require you to pay an extra tax or apply for a permit to be a host on Airbnb. If you're required to collect tax, clearly state this in your listing and charge guests by using the Special Offer feature in the messaging center or roll the cost into your price per night. Also note that Airbnb will give hosts a Form 1099 at year's end, so you may need to declare earnings on your tax returns. Note also there are deductions available for rental expenses. It is always best to consult with your tax preparer beforehand.

Insurance

You should check your home insurance to make sure you're covered for any situations involving paid guests. Airbnb also provides for a "host guarantee" of up to $1M. See website FAQs for details. Further note that if you do not own your living space you may not be able to be an Airbnb host.

Search Rankings

These are determined by your 90-day activity, guest reviews, message responses, and availability calendar updates.

Communications

Airbnb advises that all communications with your guests be done through the website to create a paper trail. You can also do a voice connect within Airbnb.

Credits

If you refer friends to Airbnb and they participate either as a host or a guest, both you and they will receive credits for Airbnb stays.

"How I Lived Rent Free Using Airbnb.com"

by Chelsea Rustrum

Around the time I first moved to San Francisco, I got hit by the double whammy of seeing my expenses increase while my revenues got cut in half. Since I'm an internet entrepreneur by trade, Google dictates how well I do to one extent or another. Without boring you with the details, let's just say that my web traffic went down by 60% overnight, all due to an algorithm update concerning search results. Google is constantly updating the way that websites are ranked and, unfortunately, mine got mixed in with other content sites that were dubbed "spammy". Unfortunately, my website wasn't. But the deed was done and that meant I suddenly couldn't afford my new apartment or my new life.

Losing half my income necessitated cutting expenses across the board. This meant having little to no social life and definitely not buying any new clothes. Even so, I soon realized I just couldn't live this way and, as a hard-core entrepreneur, I wasn't about to take a 9-to-5 job out of desperation.

So, what to do? I found even more creative ways to both save money and generate new income. Somehow and somewhat counterintuitively, all of this actually started making for a more exciting life. I shopped at farmers markets and recycled clothing stores. I rode buses or walked instead of taking taxis. I'd also met fellow author Gabriel and started hanging out at his collective and pitching in on meal nights.

As for new revenue streams, I put my couch up for rent on Airbnb for $35 a night. Initially I was just curious, but within hours

I'd received several requests. And what astonished me most was the amount of detail and personalized attention that people put into their requests. It seemed like, wow, people wanted to pay, not only for my accommodations, but to meet me! My first guest was a gal from Chicago who wanted to expand her highly successful photo safari business to San Francisco. She was coming out here for a week to interview people and needed a place to crash.

Instantly, we clicked and I felt like I'd known her for years. I invited her to a tech event I'd been lucky enough to get free tickets for and she immediately fit in. I'll never forget how touched I was when she bought me hand soap because I'd run out. This isn't an anomaly. A subsequent guest bought me hand soap as well. Perhaps I should have learned to keep extra hand soap on hand?

Needing hand soap is no reason to join Airbnb, but the experiment proved something important. Airbnb is different from Couchsurfing in that they each attract different communities of people. Couchsurfers expect to connect and share, as they're already in that mindset. People who use Airbnb are initially drawn to the savings and convenience, but are usually pleasantly surprised when the host-guest barriers come down and they find themselves having a more personal experience than they would ever have had by staying in a hotel.

By now I've had my couch graced by countless travelers, entrepreneurs, investors, conference attendees, and people in the process of relocating. What I hear time and again from my guests is their gratitude in connecting to this new place, feeling a touch of home, and getting a sense of community.

Unique accommodations are only one benefit of the Airbnb experience. It's who you stay with that ultimately determines whether you'll have the kind of "insider" experience that can only come with the help of someone who knows the terrain. People who can otherwise afford $300 a night at the local Sheraton will opt for a $50 couch in a private apartment if they get someone who's able to enhance their visit, and perhaps share a glass of wine with at the end of the day. And couples who'd easily part with $250 per night for a room in a B&B love getting a complete private apartment with a well-stocked kitchen in a central location for half that price.

How to Setup a Coliving House

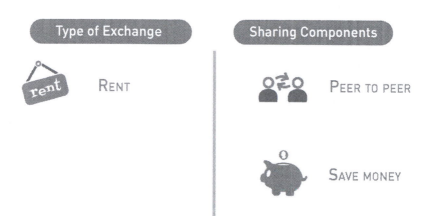

Type of Exchange

Rent

Sharing Components

Peer to peer

Save money

When you consider all the economic advantages of shared expenses, coliving can make it possible for a group of people to live in, well, a mansion with expansive grounds, multiple bedrooms with private bathrooms, a large top-of-the-line kitchen, and central dining and meeting rooms. Oh, yeah!

First, Some Definitions:

- ▶ Coliving – an arrangement where a group of like-minded individuals share the costs of living in a large apartment, house, or loft, and usually build a community around a certain concept, shared values, or ideology.
- ▶ Coworking – a shared office space set up for entrepreneurs, freelancers, consultants, and remote workers to conduct business and perform their work in a community-oriented environment.
- ▶ Cohousing – a community where people live in separate dwellings with a common area for group meetings and social interactions.

What is Coliving?

While coliving might conjure up images of life in a fraternity house, there are distinctions. Coliving people may have common interests, but they choose to live together based on shared values or intentions. Members are chosen for what they believe in, and they all work together to create a common vision inside the house as well as out in the world.

Coliving arrangements are popping up all over Silicon Valley and in places where the creative class is alive and well. Coliving works well for entrepreneurs, artists, innovators, yogis, technologists, and any other groups who share common goals. Typically, the arrangements are set up for people in the 25-45 age range, but all age groups can benefit from this lifestyle.

Providing the opportunity, time, and space for people to develop close and meaningful relationships can be transformational.

However, just as sharing office space is not necessarily coworking, living in the same building with housemates is not necessarily coliving. Here there are private sleeping rooms, but tasks and meals are usually shared. Also there are common meeting areas, and decisions are typically made as a group. Usually everyone in a coliving household understands and appreciates the importance of operating as a collective and contributing to the group through communal cooking, cleaning, events, outings, maintenance, up-keep, and the other necessary chores of everyday life.

Note that there are other opportunities to share living space. Cohousing, like coliving, is also an intentional community, but often involves a cluster of separate individual dwellings around a central common area. Although all "co-type" experiences can sometimes overlap, the following discussion will be limited to the simplest arrangement – coliving.

While coliving isn't necessarily just about saving money, the act of sharing space reduces costs and makes it possible to live the proverbial champagne lifestyle on a lite-beer budget. If you're lucky, there may be extra space for offices, craft or shop areas, a fitness room, or even a swimming pool and hot tub. Polo, anyone?

HOW TO SET UP A COLIVING HOUSE

STEP 1: Define Your Vision

If you're the one setting up the coliving arrangement, you will need a strong vision of the community in order to attract the right- and like-minded people. Being the originator of a group will involve hard work and often a personal financial commitment. So you will need to set clear expectations and define the practical details in order to surround yourself with people who are just as passionate as you are.

For example, if you're a chiropractor and into the healing arts, perhaps you'd want to create a house centered on the wellness community. As an entrepreneur, you might want to create an environment that emphasizes changing the world. And if you're deeply rooted into the artistic or music community, your house vision might be about creativity, design, and expression.

STEP 2: Use Facebook

Once you decide that coliving is for you, create a Facebook group to enable your potential participants to easily communicate.

Tips:

▶ Keep the Facebook group on a private setting so only you can add members

▶ Add interested people as you encounter them

▶ Schedule an in-person event to discuss living together (aim for 8-10 people to be in attendance)

STEP 3: Meet the Candidates

At the coliving house meetup, discuss people's situations, preferences, and expectations. What kind of accommodations are they are looking for? Do people want private rooms? Are they okay with shared bathrooms? How much is each person currently paying per month? How much are they willing to pay for coliving? Any geographic preferences? Transportation requirements?

Tip: You can set up a Facebook poll within the group to gather much of this information before you meet.

STEP 4: Determine the Costs

Typically with coliving, some costs are on a per room basis (as some rooms are bigger/better, some people may share rooms, etc.) and some costs are on a per person basis (utilities, food, supplies, etc.). After getting an idea of each person's budget and space requirements, you can then estimate what type and size of place you can afford.

STEP 5: Find Committed Partners

After communications within your Facebook group and after your meet up session(s), it's time to sign on the dotted line. You'll need to enroll one to three others to help with the heavy lifting of finding the place, handling the logistics, and sharing the financial responsibility. Moral support is good to have, too.

It's also a good time to test the waters to find out how many others in the group are serious about moving into the space. You will need a significant deposit to move in.

STEP 6: Locate the Space

Be prepared to spend several months to find the right coliving space. This will be the most important decision the group will make, and you'll want to handle as many of the individual "must-haves" and "nice-to-haves" as possible. You may not be able to completely satisfy everyone, but aim for the most good for the most people.

Considerations:

▶ Bedrooms/Bathrooms – should closely correlate with the number of people and their preferences

▶ Common Areas – sometimes older buildings have lots of bedrooms but don't have proper living rooms or large enough kitchens for multiple people to cook in and hang out

▶ Vibe/Feel – physical space should match group expectations – for example, if you're putting together a house for the wellness community, you probably don't want a place that smells like smoke or has very little light

▶ Location – do you need to be near public transport, freeways, restaurants, stores (check walkscore.com)? What's the parking situation like? Again, what are the stated expectations?

Tip: Continue communicating with the group regularly through the Facebook group, schedule periodic meetings, and solicit feedback and ideas – keep the momentum going!

STEP 7 : Work Out the Details

Much of this should have already been discussed and decided on upfront:

► <u>Food</u>

Will you share food? Often in communal houses, it works best if all the food is shared. Bulk food can be bought for everyone, and people with dietary restrictions can buy other food and expense it to the house. Bonding over cooking and meals is a great way to strengthen the community.

► <u>Cleaning</u>

You can create a chore wheel and assign cleaning responsibilities to be shared and changed weekly. Also consider having a house cleaner come every month to do a deep cleaning.

► <u>Supplies</u>

Many communal houses buy their supplies in bulk and expense them as part of the utilities. You can shop at warehouse stores like Costco or buy some items like toilet paper and soap from Amazon.com.

STEP 8: Establish Community Norms

A coliving arrangement is more of a living organism than just a shared house, so you'll need to be deliberate about how decisions are made, how feedback is given, how rules/expectations may change, etc. Try to be as transparent and democratic as possible, allowing the community to shape itself. But it's good to have a working document of community norms to get the group moving in the same direction.

There should also be a list of house rules specifying things like smoking, quiet hours, guests, etc., and any particular items such as "no dirty dishes on the counters" or "no shoes in the house", etc.

STEP 9: Apply for the Space(s)

Once you've located a place(s), it's time to put ink on applications. Depending on the real estate market in your area, you may want to apply for more than one place in case you don't get your first choice. You will need all committed people to sign the paperwork.

STEP 10: Secure the Space

Once you are approved, you and your partners now need to negotiate/agree to the lease terms, sign the documents, and put down the deposit – now you're getting somewhere.

STEP 11: Communicate Consistently

It's a good idea to spend time together socially and get to know each other before the move-in. The more comfortable people are with each other, the easier communicating the harder stuff will be – and move-ins can be stressful.

STEP 12: Move In!

You've made it this far – congratulations! If people are coming from the same area, consider sharing a moving truck. Try to enroll friends to help out. Sometimes free beer and pizza will do the trick, along with invitations to the upcoming house-warming party.

STEP 13: Furnish the Space

If you'll be needing things, check out the chapter on Shareable Stuff; find furniture on Craigslist, Freecycle, or second-hand stores; and ask Facebook friends for any particular items. Ask everyone in the group to bring all of their kitchenware, glasses, gadgets, cups, plates, silverware, and supplies.

Tip: If you're going to be hosting events with a decent amount of foot traffic, consider acquiring art from local artists who want to show off their work.

STEP 14: Schedule Dinners and Events

Events, events, events! Okay, you don't have to throw parties every weekend, but consistent social activity is a key to building community. If you decide on Sunday night dinners, have them every Sunday even if not everyone can make it. That way you can establish a rhythm to the household and people can plan accordingly. You can also schedule game nights, music jams, movie nights, theme parties, etc.

You can plan group activities outside the house like going to concerts, street fairs, ball games, festivals, camping, etc.

Tip: Consider having occasional potlucks where members invite their friends – these are great ways to build community, as well as scoping out new menu ideas for when it's your turn to cook.

STEP 15: Create a Website or Blog

First, name your house. This might sound cheesy, but most coliving houses are actually given a name and people do refer to them by their given names. Then set up a website on Wordpress.com or Tumblr.com to tell the world about what you're doing, announce events, and provide a way for people to contact you. Depending on the theme of your space you may want to get a blog going as well.

STEP 16: Use Social Media

There is no shame in shameless self-promotion. Put your space on the map! You could skip this step if your household is not very techie, but using social media is another way to help household members and their friends keep in the know.

Facebook Page

Now that you've thought up a totally cool name for your coliving house, gotten the website up, and started your blog, it's time to get that Facebook page. Then invite friends, colleagues, and other people who might be interested in what you're up to.

Twitter Account

Along the same lines, set up a Twitter account for the house so people can refer to the house when they're onsite, for example,

Lovin' the Community @yourhousename – "3 musicians are jamming here tonight!"

Foursquare

Add your house name into Foursquare so people can tag you and announce their location when they're at your house.

STEP 17: Steer the Ship

Empowerment

Kinda goes without saying, but remember to empower your members to have fun and share responsibility. Make people feel like they own the household decisions and have a say in how things are run. If you've put a solid structure in place and attracted people based on shared values, finding common ground shouldn't be too difficult.

Meetings

Schedule occasional house meetings to allow members to check in and discuss ongoing issues. Keep things light (provide chocolate and wine!), so that people will look forward to getting together.

Social Director

Have at least one social director to keep group activities going. Note that this is a very important contribution and should be considered equal weight when tasks are being assigned.

Be Transparent

It's important for all members to have access to all house financial information such as rent, utilities, food, maintenance, and anything else your house spends money on. Set up a binder that contains all the bills and receipts, and an accounting of who owes what. Make sure all members have a copy of the lease agreement.

STEP 18: Check the Vibes

Address Conflicts

If there is an issue in the house, be willing to face it. Sooner is better than later, and denial usually just creates more tension. As with any type of relationship, you need to be able to talk things out and come to acceptable resolutions.

Changing the Lineup

If someone is not a fit, you can ask them to leave. Check local landlord laws and regulations to make sure you're not doing anything illegal, but generally speaking if a living situation is not working, it's not working on both sides. You may have also spelled out procedures in the preliminary documentation for how members enter and leave the group.

Coliving Examples and Resources:

- ► Coliving.org: an interactive map of coliving houses
- ► Rainbow Mansion: rainbowmansion.com
- ► Embassy Network: embassynetwork.com
- ► Campus: buildcampus.com

HOW TO SHARE YOUR PARKING SPOT

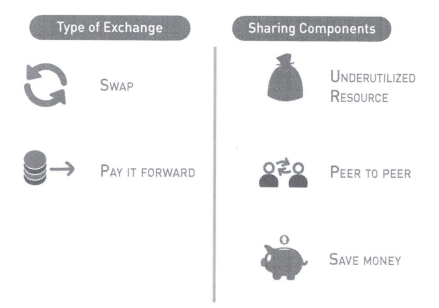

How many hours of your life have you lost just going around in circles looking for parking? It's stressful and problematic, and if you live in a city you need to be constantly aware of tow-away zones, one-hour parking meters, street cleaning times, curbs painted white or yellow or red or blue, neighborhood parking time limits, etc. The list of gotchas goes on and on.

Craigslist was the first website to allow people to rent their private parking spaces. However, that user interface leaves much to be desired in that you have to keep re-posting your ad and you can't just turn it on or off. And as a renter there is no easy way to filter for just the closest spots or available times in your neighborhood.

Parkcirca.com is an example of an easy-to-use online service that allows you to convert your unused space into cash and give your community more needed parking. Typically you can rent out your parking spot for $1-3 per hour and, say, on average of four hours per day this adds up to $120-360 per month! Park circa takes 25% of the rental fee and the owner gets the rest. Like those great philosophers Dire Straits once said, "Money for nothin'."

Other parking options include: Parkingpanda, Google's "Open Spot", Texas' Uniiverse, and there is always the old-school Craigslist way.

In the discussion below we'll use Parkcirca as an example of how you too can help create a calmer, stress-free world by sharing your parking space, or by paying to use someone else's underutilized spot to preserve your own sanity.

Perhaps you have an extra spot in the garage, space in your driveway, or won't be home for a day or a week or a month. Whatever the reason, share that spot! Since sharing parking is still a relatively new phenomenon, most of the services in the U.S. don't yet have a large inventory or a built-up demand. But that tsunami is coming soon to a neighborhood street near you.

The driving factor is demand. If you live in an urban area, especially a congested city like San Francisco, you'll have a much easier time finding harried and willing customers. If you offer it, they will come.

HOW TO SHARE YOUR PARKING SPACE

STEP 1: Create an Account

Download the app or sign up at Parkcirca.com and choose the "List a parking space" option.

You can either sign up with Facebook or create a new account with details such as your name, phone number, email address, and password. You'll also have to choose whether the account is for business, personal, or non-profit use. Unless you own your own parking lot, choose to set up a "personal" account.

STEP 2: List Your Space

▶ Address – Post the exact street address

▶ Description – Give a complete and accurate description:

Is the space in a garage? Or carport? Outdoor parking? Is there a security guard or attendant on site? Is the space in your driveway? In front of your driveway?

▶ Photo – Post a good clear photo of the space:

Grab your mobile device and take a quick shot to post to your listing.

▶ Issues – Definitely point out any limitations:

If there are restrictions on parking hours, vehicle height or length limits, any do's and don'ts, or other issues, then make sure these details are made known. When it comes to parking, surprises are, like, totally un-fun.

▶ <u>Verification</u>:

Note that Parkcirca has a verification system which ensures the spot is a legitimate space and is authorized for rent by the proper owner. Verified spaces take priority in system searches over non-verified ones. Parkcirca provides a sign that you can post at your verified spot, which will likely result in more business!

STEP 3: Set Your Price and Availability

Specify the hours and days that your space is available. Additionally you can specify availability in real time. Note that you can also set dynamic parking rates based on day of the week and/or hours of the day. You can list daily, weekly, and monthly rates.

Tip: You can opt to receive email or text message notifications to your smartphone whenever someone checks in or out of your space.

Tip: If a driver does not leave the space by the agreed time, you can have them towed and they will be responsible for all fees. However, since you have each others' contact info, this should not be necesary.

STEP 4: Rate Your Driver, er, Parker

Like all other self-regulating services within the sharing economy, writing reviews is the best way to build reputation and trust.

STEP 5: Get Paid!

If you're renting out your extra parking spot for less than a month, you'll pay 25% of fees earned to Parkcirca for providing the service. You may request payment at the end of each month or keep the money in your account to use as your credit for parking elsewhere.

For monthly parking, Parkcirca can handle your billing. This saves you from having to process your own payments, write leases, and more. For that, you will pay them 10% of whatever revenue you generate monthly as a service fee. However, listing monthly parking is free and you're allowed to handle billing on your own if you want to.

OTHER WAYS TO SHARE YOUR HOME

What about sharing your yard, your garage, or even your bathroom? As you saw in the Shareable Stuff chapter, there are platforms now that allow you to share just about anything in your home from your digital camera, whitewater kayak, and even those boxes of old baby clothes. Maybe we were just kidding about your bathroom.

Also consider that the unused patch of ground in your backyard could sprout into a community garden through websites like sharedearth.com (see the Shareable Food chapter). And let's not forget the 10% of the U.S. population that has to rent a storage unit. So why not put that empty corner of your garage to good use? You can rent it out through sharemystorage.com or roost.com.

Even Shareable Dogs

And how about your pooch? Would you share your dog with a neighbor who wanted a doggie play-date, or a jogging companion, or just some fluffy-eared face time?

Your dog probably spends a lot of time just hanging around the house. But now there are new ways you can share your furry friend. Websites like dogvacay.com and rover.com have emerged, allowing everyday people to take in and board other people's dogs while they are away on vacation. Citydogshare.org is a free pet-sitting co-op now operating through Facebook groups in San Francisco, Denver, Phoenix, Portland, Seattle, and San Diego – and if you don't see your area listed, put in a request to start one up in your location. The service matches owners having dog "down-times" with people who'd enjoy taking a dog along on their next walk in the park, etc.

Living a Sharable Life

"The new economy puts more value in relationships than in stuff."

- Chelsea Rustrum
Co-author of It's a Shareable Life

Sharing for a Flexible Lifestyle
by Chelsea Rustrum

I began tinkering with websites when I was 14 years old, and by age 16 I'd accidentally stumbled on to a lucrative web business. However, even though I was already successful, I felt like college was the only true way to prove my ability and intelligence to the world. So, seven years later, I finally graduated with a degree in business from Cal Poly.

I desperately tried to fit into the standard life equation of "Education plus Job plus Marriage equals Happiness." But when I realized this wasn't the equation for my happiness, I quit my job, packed my bags, and headed out for my first six-month adventure as a wandering entrepreneur. I decided that I wasn't ready for marriage either and, cliché or not, I needed to find myself. Although I didn't know exactly what I was doing or where I was going, I did know I had to see, feel, learn, and experience more of the world.

On the Road, and Back

The journey through Southeast Asia and Australia was magical. I stayed in hostels and guesthouses and met travelers from all over who fired my imagination with interesting stories about faraway places. By the time I was ready to come back, I felt grounded enough to restart my life as a young adult. Take Two, or "once more with feeling."

Upon returning, I learned that a friend had started NextSpace Coworking (read: a homebase for isolated entrepreneurs). Since I'd just been months on the road, the idea of having some stability really appealed to me. I dug both feet into the turf of this new shared office environment.

At NextSpace I made friends quickly. Though I had my own office, I always felt like I was part of something bigger. As every person was participating, we slowly built the coworking space into a community. At first none of us realized it, but this was what we'd wanted all along – to connect, to create, and to support each other in our individual endeavors. Some of us even began collaborating on projects together. It was that kind of place.

That said, about a year later the travel bug snuck up on me again, and I booked a trip to Italy on a whim. What I thought would be a two-week look-see around Rome and Florence ended up being a three-month adventure through Italy, Spain, and Germany. This was where I discovered the power and glory of Couchsurfing.

Enter Couchsurfing

Through Couchsurfing, I met so-called strangers from all over the world and we came together for happy hours, shared meals, and walk-abouts. I did everything from lake trips with locals to a four-day journey to Cinque Terre with some Couchsurfers I'd known for less than 48 hours.

Couchsurfing provided a beautiful intersection of online/offline community like I'd never experienced before. This group of international travelers was interested in living joyously, experiencing different cultures, meeting new people, and widening their worldview.

Upon returning from this soul-filled adventure, I was offered a compelling job to open and run a coworking space in San Jose, California. NextSpace needed help growing and I loved everything the company stood for, but I loved my freedom more. I couldn't imagine a 9-to-5 job with two weeks off in the summer to travel. And that's how Startup Abroad was born. I decided to marry my love for travel, coworking, and entrepreneurship together and founded Startup Abroad, which provides entrepreneurs the opportunity to live, work, and travel to international destinations as a group of ten or more.

As I discovered more about my passion for coworking, traveling far and wide, and exploring future projects, I couldn't get Couchsurfing out of my head. The irony was, even with millions of Couchsurfing members worldwide, many of my friends had never heard of it. I felt the Couchsurfing experience deserved a wider audience, and so I started bugging my filmmaker friends to cover the story.

Days after relocating to San Francisco, I had a serendipitous meeting with Alexandra Liss, an aspiring documentary filmmaker and eventual co-author of this book. Coincidentally enough, I learned she was off in five days to shoot an international Couchsurfing documentary. Within an hour of meeting her, I asked how I could help with the project. Her response? "Meet me in Europe in one month." And so I did. We filmed throughout France, Spain, and Morocco, sleeping on couches all the way.

Something More

Now that I'd gotten involved in coworking, Couchsurfing, and traveling, I began to realize there was a movement here which was bigger than the sum of its parts. Something about people helping people and accomplishing more together than they could have done individually. It was about living at a higher level, connecting the spaces in between, and utilizing more efficiently resources, time, and space. I began to envision a future where people could find community in the many different ways now being made possible by technology and mobile communications.

And that's when I reconnected with Airbnb and within one month I was living rent free. I passed on the details to my friends and within three months nearly all of them were living rent free as well.

Around this time Alexandra, Gabriel, and I began having discussions about what we called the sharing economy, in which people could lead more socially connected, financially secure, and meaningful lives. The ways and means of the sharing economy were expanding rapidly, coinciding with the widening reach of peer-to-peer platforms, evolving technologies, social media, and mobile devices that fit in your pocket. We began to get excited about the current possibilities and the potential growth of this movement. All of which ultimately led us to write this book, so that you too might be able to get in on the ground floor of leading a more rewarding life.

A SHAREABLE HOUSEHOLD
by Gabriel Stempinski

I've long been a believer in service bartering. It's a lot more common than most people realize. Ask any dentist or plumber or other skilled professional if they trade work with other professionals, and you'll be surprised to see how many of them do. My mother, for example, works as a naturopathic doctor and massage therapist and trades work "in kind" for much of her dental and medical care. One of the benefits of these arrangements is that services rendered in trade are not taxed – no money changes hands and each party gets to set the value of their services each time.

Now I understand that service trades can't be used everywhere because sometimes I need something from someone but they have no use for what I have to offer. That's why there's this other thing called money. But I do believe that we should start to consider bartering when it is a viable option.

My Service Bartering Example

At one point, I lived in a fairly large loft in San Francisco with three bedrooms, a large gourmet kitchen, two bathrooms, two parking spaces, and a 900 square foot private rooftop deck. That's a whole lotta home for just a dude and his cat, and frankly it was getting a bit lonely since my cat isn't much of a conversationalist. One night I found myself sitting alone in my big digs with my lazy cat sleeping in another room (some companion he was!) when I decided to try something new: I would get a roommate. But after six years in San Francisco I didn't want to just "rent" the room – I wanted to trade room and board for some valuable service.

Hmm, I figured a bedroom in my loft in my neighborhood was easily worth $1,200 a month on the open market, and if I really pitched it I could probably get $1,500. So, I posted an ad on Craigslist and searched other classifieds. I got a few interesting responses, mostly from students willing to do personal assistant type work for me. But I'm a pretty simple dude and I handle most of the administrative stuff for my business myself. An accountant offered to do my taxes for the room, but my quarterlies usually only cost me $450 three times a year, so that math wasn't going to work. Plus, I love the accountant I have.

It wasn't until I checked my Couchsurfing account one day and remembered there was a "roommate" subgroup. I saw an ad from a fitness trainer and cook (she had references) looking for a room, and she was offering a complimentary gym membership, personal training, weight counseling, and healthy cooking, along with $400 per month in rent money. Hmm, again. I had just wrapped up a five-month project in Europe and, thanks to my love of French food and Belgian beer, had packed on 20 pounds. The thought of having someone to cook healthy food and get me back into shape was appealing. I did the math. Maria's offer of the gym membership (worth $50-100 a month in San Francisco) and personal training (worth $600-1,000 a month, assuming ten sessions per month) already made it well worthwhile for me. To top it off she insisted on paying the $400 a month rent even though I said her fitness training was more than enough. Plus, the frosting on the cake (which, BTW, I was no longer eating) was that she was an excellent cook and she made sure there was always delicious, healthy food in the house.

So on my side, I felt like I was getting an amazing bargain. I would easily be spending over \$2,000 a month to buy the equivalent services. In return Maria felt that she was getting an incredible deal because she wasn't doing much more than she would be doing otherwise for herself. I would cover the grocery bills and she would get a room in a great location with all the creature comforts she was looking for. All this in exchange for conducting a couple of weekly training sessions and providing a few minutes of daily good-natured badgering at me to stick to my routines. To top it all off, I now have a great friend and someone to make the loft feel a lot less "empty." My cat even likes her too.

I've also started using airbnb.com to rent out the other unused bedroom and occasionally the couch (which is usually reserved for Couchsurfers). This brings in between \$1,500 and \$3,000 per month, and I'm making even more friends as well since many of the Airbnb-ers and Couchsurfers have been young professionals in the process of relocating to the city.

A Happy Ending

So there you have it. I went from being a slightly chubby and fairly unhealthy dude living alone in a big empty loft to being a fairly healthy guy who can now fit back into his pre-Europe clothes. I share my unused space with great people, eat healthy food, and make an extra couple of grand a month to sweeten the deal.

If I were to fully monetize the earning potential of my loft on Airbnb, it would be easily over \$4,000 a month. And I'm not even an extreme hosting example. Many others are able to completely cover all their expenses by sharing their living space. So whether you're a starving artist tired of starving or a professional with a spare bedroom, you can benefit directly and indirectly by stepping up your game and creating a shareable household.

SHARING TO CREATE LUCK
by Alexandra Liss

People always tell me, "You are SO lucky!"

I did not grow up rich or acquire a trust fund. But, I was still able to Couchsurf through 6 continents, 21 countries, shoot and edit an indie documentary. And I continue to live like the nouveau riche: traveling when I please, working from where I want to, having drivers, free cars, free rent, free furniture, free clothes, bartered luxuries -- all while making below the median income. So what is the catch? Am I just lucky? Nah.

Enthusiasm + like minded community = LUCK.

I regularly use TaskRabbit, rent my place on Airbnb, purchase second-hand goods off of Craigslist, share my car on GetAround and spend less money on stuff by using Yerdle. Plus, I participate in clothing swaps and gift my time by helping other filmmakers.

Regularly putting myself out there puts me in contact with new opportunities and people I never would have met if didn't lead a life rich in sharing who I am, requesting help and providing assistance to others. The more I experiment and follow my enthusiasm, giving at every chance I can, the more luck-filled my life becomes.

The "not-so-secret-sharing-sauce" to having a luck-filled existence is not random. We design each and every one of our opportunities by following our greatest enthusiasms and talents, and by surrounding ourselves with those (via platforms and in person) who have mutual enthusiasm and willingness to share. Luckily, these tech platforms are making it easier and easier to connect with that essential ingredient of like-minded community. When you do that, serendipity and abundance inevitably follow.

By leading a Shareable Life, I've created breeding ground for serendipity and connection and because of that, luck is everywhere I look.

Using the Sharing Economy to Get Out of Debt
featuring Sarah Peck

From the outside, Sarah Peck seemed to have it all – a plush job at a Sausalito architectural firm, a burgeoning career in communications and design, a masters degree in Landscape Architecture from Penn, and an ever-curious, bubbly personality. But you wouldn't know she'd been struggling for years to get out of debt.

Peck explains, "No one knew that I wore the same black dress over and over because I couldn't afford new clothes. I'd even dodge cameras at parties."

And she goes on to add, "People believed I had it all going on because of my blog where I write about people leading the lives they've always wanted. My reality was that I was living in a garage to pay off the $75,000 debt I'd incurred getting my graduate degree."

Sarah began using services like Getaround, Airbnb, and clothing swaps with friends to lead a simpler life that enabled her to become completely debt-free in just one year. She earned $200+ a month renting out her car to neighbors on Getaround, rented the extra space in her current three bedroom apartment on Airbnb, and traded clothes with five girlfriends who happen to be the same size.

The clothing swap was largely informal, but worked out well. One friend of Sarahs's typically dropped off a bag at Sarah's so she could go through and take what she wanted, add pieces she no longer wore, and then pass it all on to the next friend.

Sarah loves the movement toward shared resources. "We've lost many of our natural ways of connecting. We're shuttered in silos of technology, working long hours, and lacking the natural serendipity and spontaneity that make life exciting. Accidentally crossing paths doesn't happen as much when we drive our own cars, telecommute, and watch a TV that doesn't talk back. With all these diminished interactions, it's no wonder people are so depressed and overweight."

When asked why she believes in sharing and uses it in her daily life, Sarah responded, "Money flies out of our hands when we believe we need to buy all of these things. I've been able to share things, save money, and connect with people more deeply."

Today, Sarah is happily out of debt and recently returned from traveling the world with her new husband. She now resides in New York City, and works for herself as a writer, storyteller, and designer - inspiring others to write and live their dreams. You can find out more at itstartswith.com.

SHARING TO TRAVEL MORE
featuring Kate Kendall

Kate Kendall is a culture hacker, explorer, sharing economy enthusiast, and an entrepreneur in the digital space. She was born in England but grew up in Australia, and recently decided to base her growing business in the U.S. She also founded thefetch.com, a weekly email digest that helps professionals find and share events that are relevant to their careers. With roots in community building and social media strategy, Kate has recently co-founded a new company called CloudPeeps, which enables companies to hire community managers who work remotely (so they can travel of course).

Kate loves the hacking life. She's been a "digital nomad" living full-time as an Airbnb guest for the past few years, only recently creating a home base in New York City. She still travels a lot for work and play, but never without renting her space in the lucrative NYC market while she's away. When Kate moved into her new apartment, she hired a TaskRabbit to help her pick up furniture from IKEA in Brooklyn and then assemble them for her (as she had none of the proper tools to do this herself).

She has also taught community-building classes for Skilshare and General Assembly. These classes have helped her to become a better public speaker and to feel more connected in the new cities she visits. Mentoring website clarity.fm is another service she frequently uses to help share her knowledge. Here budding entrepreneurs from all over the globe can call up a mentor like Kate to get expert advice and guidance over the phone, all for a small fee.

If anyone understands how the sharing economy helps you live a more flexible lifestyle, it's Kate. "I love the concept of 'pay as you go' living for ultimate agility. Without the freedom afforded by the sharing economy, I wouldn't be the person I am or in the position I'm in today. It's completely changed my life – giving me the fluidity to evolve and be in the moment. I don't think I was truly conscious or fully living before."

"The sharing economy has helped me stay true to the essence of humanity. Ultimately it's the people, experiences, impact, and giving that matter – not acquiring stuff or spending time doing things that don't fulfill you."

"Nick Just Wants to Help"

featuring Nick Crawford

In 2008 Nick began his journey into the sharing economy through Couchsurfing. Nick's wife, an avid traveler, talked him into hosting guests in their home in Milwaukee. "We'd gone to Nicaragua for our honeymoon instead of Costa Rica, and we had more fun and ended up with better stories. Cruise ships are great, but we'd rather hack it and do something more adventurous."

At one point, Nick was a TaskRabbit, a Sidecar driver, and used ride sharing services like Zimride to find riders and earn a little extra cash on his road trips. As Nick explains, "Sharing feels like the stuff I have is more than mine."

Starting with TaskRabbit

When Nick and his wife moved from Milwaukee to San Francisco, he had to quickly find a way to earn an income. "I started doing TaskRabbit after I'd turned down other job opportunities for $20 an hour which wasn't quite enough to support my family in the city." Nick had heard about the TaskRabbit service and hired a TaskRabbit worker to paint their home. The TaskRabbit was a "no-show" and Nick thought, "I can do better than that. I don't think anyone should ever flake on a customer."

Two weeks after submitting his online application and ace-ing his video interview, Nick was off to the races as a TaskRabbit. "I decided to bill myself out for $15 an hour at first, just to get started." Nick's first task was picking up a load of rocks from Home Depot and delivering them to someone's house. "When I got there the woman was sweet and had a German accent. I off-loaded the rocks to her back yard, and then this one job turned into a week of work doing a full landscape of her front yard. And on top of my fee, she gave me a $100 tip. I was floored. I also realized I wasn't charging enough."

After that, Nick started bidding on projects at $30 per hour, and was getting half of the jobs he bid on. Later on, he was bidding at $65 per hour and still winning half of the bids. "People usually go with whatever they can afford. By going higher, people feel like they are getting higher quality."

When asked why he worked as a TaskRabbit, Nick explains, "At first I used the service primarily to make money. There is a wide variety of short-term gigs you can do in the city, but I think many of those are less rewarding. I need the immediate gratification of completing a job and making someone happy. I enjoy creating something beautiful, or even better – that's one of the best things about TaskRabbit."

Once Nick finally settled into San Francisco life he got a full-time sales job similar to what he did in Milwaukee. He still occasionally picks up TaskRabbit jobs and does recurring work for previous customers, but now he's mostly focused on his new gig.

Other Work Options

However, the new job doesn't keep Nick from being a Sidecar driver on some evenings. He feels technology makes it easy for anyone to be a driver. "You don't have to be a local or an insider. I'd only been in the city for three months when I started driving, and with the navigation app I'm a guru of the city streets." Asked about his motives for driving, Nick replies, "If money is your only reason for driving, it's going to be less rewarding. But if you like talking to people and getting to know your way around the city, then I think Sidecar driving is pretty much perfect."

Nick has had experiences where he's weaved several sharing economy services together. The first was a combo with TaskRabbit and Zimride.

Nick tells us, "It was a slow day for TaskRabbit yard work, so I looked in the Moving section. Someone needed children's furniture moved from San Francisco to Reno. I bid and won the task at $275 roundtrip. It was four hours each way and I volunteered to drive my own vehicle. My wife was upset that I'd agreed to take our car, put extra miles on it, and burn up all that gas. I felt like I had to prove myself and validate my efforts."

So a few days before leaving, Nick joined Zimride and posted the ride share to Reno. "I got a bunch of responses. The longer the trip, the more people you get matched up with. I could only take one rider on the way there because the back seat would be full of furniture. I opted for the most straightforward and flexible person, a guy who was a ski instructor in the winter and worked for the family landscaping company in the summer. This made for a great ride out there." On the way back, Nick picked up two more passengers and earned $25 per passenger. After returning to San Francisco, Nick did a two-hour job for a repeat TaskRabbit customer.

All in a days work: $275 for the furniture moving, $75 for the ride sharing, and another $88 for the recurring task. So for ten hours of sharing economy work, Nick earned a total of $438.

That's $43.80 an hour! And the TaskRabbit customer whose furniture Nick moved from San Francisco to Reno spoke to him on the phone afterwards for a total of three minutes and then reviewed him with, "Nick just wants to help."

We think that's pretty accurate.

Final Thoughts

The economy of connection and interdependence

Known as everything from collaborative consumption to the peer-to-peer economy, we hope the future sharing economy will no longer need a name and will simply be referred to as "the economy."

The authors of this guidebook consider the sharing economy to be a peer-to-peer revolution and a truly democratizing movement, which puts power back into the hands of individuals. This represents an avenue to a newfound sense of freedom and a way for people to access unique and meaningful experiences. And let's be real - the sharing economy gives people a flexible way to remain employed, even in a down economy.

We hope this book gives you new perspective, a renewed faith in humanity, and understanding of how interdependence can play an integral role in the new economy. This movement about people being more human with each other, sharing what they have access to, and mutually benefiting along the way.

The future of sharing

Since the sharing economy is changing everything, the authors have some predictions for what might happen next and maybe even a new vision for how we'd like to see the future...

Our Vision for the Future:

▶ People will have equal access to education, generating a more global, egalitarian economy

▶ There will be more communal housing and blurred lines between work, play, and raising a family

▶ Shared self-driving cars will get us where we need to go, rendering the necessity of car ownership obsolete

▶ Work will be flexible and enable more people to work remotely from anywhere

▶ People will increasingly move to urban areas, own fewer possessions, and live smarter in less space

▶ There will be a tighter kinship between neighbors and more localized sharing, fueled by technology and grassroots efforts

▶ Cities and municipalities will integrate sharing services into the fabric of everyday life, becoming "sharing cities"

▶ Truly peer-driven organizations will emerge, generating shared ownership amongst the providers with open source software and hybrid legal models

▶ An internationally networked value exchange will enable people to lend their homes, cars, and possessions without currency

We know there will be challenges, setbacks, and hiccups as policy makers struggle to make sense of the new economy, but we're confident the sharing economy is going to change life as we know it for the better.

Final wish for our readers

Bigger picture aside, our goal is to help you see that you can live a life dictated by choice, passion, and freedom - a life where your shared experiences are of the highest value.

We hope that you see how the sharing economy can fuel your next adventure, provide new opportunities, and completely transform your life!

Please share this book and visit us at ShareableLife.com

DEDICATION

Firstly, we'd like to thank every single person who made this book possible through supporting our Kickstarter crowdfunding campaign - all 136 of you.

We'd also like to shout out to the TaskRabbits who edited some of the content, our 99 Designs expert, Audrey who brought the feel of the book to life, and to all of the sharing gurus who gave us valuable ideas, feedback, and allowed their stories to be told. The sharing economy is truly what what made this book possible!

Thank you also to Jeremy Neuner for always giving us honest feedback, Kathleen Haff for editing throughout the night, James James Redenbaugh for being the light at the 11th hour of design changes, Rachel Botsman for remaining supportive throughout, and to Neal Gorenflo for championing the sharing economy and setting the tone for this book.

This book is dedicated to all human beings connecting more deeply - and to people trusting one another to help each other get their needs met. This book is dedicated to rebuilding the economy in sustainable ways in which we can all benefit and be proud.

After spending two years doing sharing experiments, our goal is to show you that the sharing economy really is truly revolutionary; on an individual level you can save or make money and have amazing experiences, and at a collective level these peer-to-peer exchanges are redefining the very structure of our economy. We urge you to take the ideas in this book seriously, and try a few of them so that you can see what we've seen: the sharing economy makes all of us richer.

Thanks very much to all of our backers, including:

Chris Curtis, Matt Johnston, Tom Currier, Jeffrey Hunt, Douglas Crets, Blake Wirht, Hope Leman, Jeremy Neuner, Desi Danganan, Karen Lai, Enzo Lombard, SD LE Consulting Inc., Jessica Carlson, Curtis James Tilleraas, Eric Werbalowsky, Ray Podder, Sultan Saeed Al Darmaki, Chris Lin, Antony Evans, Rob Modzelewski, Abe Cajudo, Mr. Shantyboat, Amanda de Luis, Jason Tam, Joshua James, David Lang, Teresa Gonczy, Cody Fale, Ryan Bethencourt, Zach Cole, Jonathan Yankovich, Augusto Camargo, Jonathon Kresner, Luna Jaffe, Kate Kendall, Ertan Dogrultan, Rusty Lindgren, Denise Wakeman, Aleksandra Sasha Markova, Robert Martinez, Lisa Radespiel, Alissa Reiter, Adam Jorlen, Monique Llamas, William Marshall, Jorren Schauwaert, Alex Grafetsberger, Maria Pazos Garcia- Camino, Ibon Doval, Ser Colin Maudry, Ian MacKenzie, John Roberts, Micah Silverman, Fanny Delahalle, Lars Christensen, Jonathan Smith, Mayel de Borniol, Damon Anderson, Alex Avery, Robyn Laing, Elatia Harris, Charles Henden, Casey Fenton, Danice Akiyoshi, Susie Lima, Brent Dixon, Zac Apte, Vijay Thirumalai, Eoin McMillan, Torsten Kolind, Adam Rofer, Pete Eakle, Kevin Hsu, Alaska Casey, Kim Dowd, Jake Tital, Jennifer Vera, Bertrand Cariou, Daniel Stern, Elizabeth Nelson, Jin Zhou, Brooke Dean, Hans Schoenburg, Gilles Samoun, Len Powell, David Anderson, Dimitris Psaropoulos, Bob Banner, C Alverson, Caterina Rindi, Jeremiah Grafsgaard, Adam Spector, Josh Schwartzman, Drew Meyers, Verwaerde Pascal, Philip Campbell, Berit Kentta-Brown, Zach Cohen, Ryan Singer, Sean Kolk, Patrick Schmidt, Maia Smith, Hans Yeakel, Nancy Grover, April Rinne, Bradley Wilson, Chad Perry, Jesse Biroscak, Breanna Wigle Hunt, Christopher J Girdwood, Jay Standish, Douglas Crets, Blake Wirht, Kathleen K Haff, Josef Dunne, and Ali Binazir.

And a special shout out goes out to BlaBlaCar, Sidecar, and Microsoft Bizspark for believing in sharing and backing the book.

Now get out there and share!

ABOUT THE AUTHORS

Chelsea Rustrum

Chelsea grew up with the internet, building websites from a young age, witnessing the evolution of the globally connected culture she always knew was possible. She's passionate about growing the movement of sharing and in revealing what she calls "our inherent interdependence." She lives in San Francisco, and has shared nearly everything covered in this book. She's an entrepreneur, a marketing consultant, and a digi-hippie at heart.

Gabriel Stempinski

Gabriel is a life adventurer, a business consultant, a father of two, and an avid Couchsurfer. He has had a wildly successful career, but has always found solace in connecting with others and in being generous. He sees no logical reason not to share and regularly buys strangers coffee, pays their bridge tolls, and generally passes on the spirit of goodwill to others. He now lives with his wife and two kids in Southern California, and is excited to see how far and wide the vision for this book can spread.

Alexandra Liss

Alexandra is a talented filmmaker. She found the sharing economy through Couchsurfing, which prompted her to crowdfund, film, and edit her first full feature documentary "One Couch at a Time," which tells the story of traveling the world for 6 months, staying on strangers' couches along the way. She's an avid sharer, regularly hosting international guests and testing the limits of what it means to share. She also lives in San Francisco, and claims to be the "unoffical mayor" having grown up in the city.

Our Story Together

Chelsea, Gabriel, and Alexandra met through the serendpity of life and the sharing economy itself. They'd all had magical experiences connecting with people internationally through Couchsurfing and had the idea to tell the story more vividly through film. Alexandra knew Gabriel from the local Couch-surfing group in San Francisco, and met Chelsea by random happenstance in a pub shortly after she'd moved to the city. The three decided to collaborate on the film "One Couch at a Time," and became fast friends through their sharing economy experiments after the filming was complete.

Chelsea, Alexandra, and Gabriel all had yearnings to spread the ideaology of the sharing economy to as many places as possible, reaching far beyond on the boundaries of the Silicon Valley.

It's a Shareable Life was born after dozens of conversations about how these services (the ideas and stories in this book) fundamentally and forever changed the lives of all three of its authors. Have we inspired you enough to go out and create your own tranformative experiences?

Made in the USA
Lexington, KY
03 April 2015